Residential Special Education

Open University Press
Children With Special Needs Series

Editors

PHILLIP WILLIAMS
Emeritus Professor of Education
University College of North Wales, Bangor.

PETER YOUNG
Formerly Tutor in the education of children with
learning difficulties, Cambridge Institute of Education;
educational writer, researcher and consultant.

This is a series of short and authoritative introductions for parents, teachers, professionals and anyone concerned with children with special needs. The series will cover the range of physical, sensory, mental, emotional and behavioural difficulties, and the changing needs from infancy to adult life in the family, at school and in society. The authors have been selected from their wide experience and close professional involvement in their particular fields. All have written penetrating and practical books readily accessible to non-specialists.

TITLES IN THE SERIES

Changing Special Education
Wilfred K. Brennan
Curriculum for Special Needs
Wilfred K. Brennan
The Early Years
Maurice Chazan and Alice Laing
Residential Special Education
Ted Cole
Working With Parents
Cliff Cunningham and Hilton Davis
Understanding Learning Difficulties
Kathleen Devereux
Special Education: The Way Ahead
John Fish

Deaf-Blind Infants and Children
J.M. McInnes and J.A. Treffry
Educating Hearing-Impaired Children
Michael Reed
Helping the Maladjusted Child
Dennis Stott
The Teacher is the Key
Kenneth Weber
How to Reach the Hard to Teach
Paul Widlake
Special Education in Minority Communities
Philip Willams (ed.)
Dyslexia or Illiteracy?
Peter Young and Colin Tyre

In preparation

Special Parents
Barbara Furneaux

Educating the Gifted Child
Joan Freeman

Beyond Childhood
Robin Jackson

Residential Special Education

Living and Learning In a Special School

Ted Cole

Open University Press

Milton Keynes · Philadelphia

Open University Press
Open University Educational Enterprises Limited
12 Cofferidge Close
Stony Stratford
Milton Keynes MK11 1BY, England
and
242 Cherry Street
Philadelphia, PA 19106. USA

First Published 1986

Copyright © Ted Cole 1986

British Library Cataloguing in Publication Data
Cole, Ted
  Residential special education: the current and future
  roles for special boarding schools.—(Children with special
  needs series)
  1. Exceptional children—Education—Great Britain
  2. Boarding schools—Great Britain
  I. Title   II. Series
  371.9'0941   LC3986.G7

  ISBN 0-335-15125-6
  ISBN 0-335-15124-8 Pbk

Library of Congress Cataloging in Publication Data
Cole, Ted.
  Residential special education.
  (Children with special needs series)
  Bibliography: p.
  1. Handicapped children—Institutional care—Great
Britain. 2. Boarding schools—Great Britain.
3. Handicapped children—Education—Great Britain.
I. Title. II. Series.
HV890.G7C65 1986   362.4'088054   86-8569
ISBN 0-335-15125-6
ISBN 0-335-15124-8 (pbk.)

Typeset by Mathematical Composition Setters Ltd, Salisbury, UK
Printed in Great Britain at The Alden Press, Oxford

Contents

Series Editors' Introduction

In the pantheon of educational mythology the angels are on the side of the integration of the handicapped and the devils are segregationists' who would pack the worst handicapped and most maladjusted pupils off to remote residential schools. Perhaps in no area of education are feelings, opinions and practices more confused and ambivalent than in the residential sector.

In England our misnamed public schools are status symbols of privilege, elitism and academic excellence. But, for the majority of the population, residential education carries the stigma of workhouse, reformitory, Borstal or Dotheboys Hall. Despite this dichotomy, many parents and voluntary bodies have laboured to set up residential schools for deaf, blind, cerebral palsied and other handicapped or orphaned children so that their needs might best be met. Special boarding schools have been seen as the best way of concentrating specialist resources, aids, therapies and skills upon handicapped children.

But even some of our outstanding achievements in meeting the needs of these pupils has met with criticisms. We recall the former pupil of a residential school for the blind saying: 'I was given a superb education — away from my parents and family, away from my contemporaries and community. Now I'm a highly qualified, highly paid executive and a complete social misfit. The only world I was fitted for was the world of the blind.' Similar complaints have been made by deaf and other sensorily impaired young people. One physically handicapped clergyman explained that he was not only being urged to work hard all the time to overcome his disabilities but his boarding school also demanded that he work hard to compensate for them by his academic achievements. 'My school life was dominated by the puritan work ethic!' he protested. 'No one gave my emotional and social development a moment's thought.'

Of course, those educated at public school also blame their education for their social isolation, marital problems, political ineptitude and much else besides — and make sure that they've got their sons' names down for their old schools. In the Soviet Union residential education is still regarded as 'a good thing' for the gifted and the handicapped alike. The USA has Public Law 94-142 which requires school boards to integrate the handicapped 'in the least restrictive environment'. In some instances this has resulted in more handicapped children getting a better and more integrated education. In others, the results have been so bad that parents have rescued their children with their pocket-books and bought private residential education.

In the real world, then, the situation is neither black and white nor blue and red. Like life, the issues and practices of special boarding education are complex and confusing. Often it seems as if, in the words of W.B. Yeats, 'The best lack all conviction, while the worst are full of passionate intensity'. Fortunately, in writing this book, Ted Cole is on neither side. What emerges is that the only side he is on is that of the children, their parents and the teachers, care staff and other professionals concerned with them.

In meeting the needs of pupils we need a sense of the mean, a sense of balance and proportion. While reading this book we have been continuously impressed by the skill and objectivity with which Ted Cole marshalls the arguments, parades the evidence, illuminates with case histories and instances, reviews the research and, where they are available, gives facts, figures and costs. Although his writing, like his own school, founded by his father, reflects his own experience and his concern for those life-enhancing qualities of tolerance, warmth and encouragement, he makes it quite clear that boarding education is a 'pragmatic second best'. But he also shows how, for some pupils, residential special education can be 'the least restrictive environment' and a lifeline to independent living and tomorrow's joy. For all their acknowledged shortcomings, there are boarding schools which have given some people the only homes, the only support and the only success they have known. As adults they return to them after service overseas, to introduce their husbands or wives and their children, or for help and advice in times of difficulties.

This book also provides a valuable examination of how these schools may be improved. As one of the founders of the Association of Independent Residential Special Schools, of which he has been chairman, Ted Cole has always striven for excellence and quality. Both the academic and care curricula receive detailed attention and it is refreshing to note the stress he places on in-service professional development, career structure and the importance of caring for the care-givers.

This is an important and thoughtful examination of theory and practice, of research evidence and of the day-to-day work of special residential schools. It points to the lessons we can learn from past and present and to the work that needs to be done. Its frank examination of problems and deficiencies helps us to see the relevant issues more clearly and in greater detail. So equipped, we are better able to make the right decisions for pupils, to advise parents, to identify suitable schools and to ensure that schools develop more flexible and effective ways of meeting pupils' needs and of bridging the gaps between school and home, community, work and pupils' futures.

Phillip Williams
Peter Young

Abbreviations and Descriptive Labels Used in the Text

ASL   American Sign Language
BDA   British Deaf Association
BM   Behaviour Modification
BSL   British Sign Language
CCETSW   Central Council for Education and Training in Social
           Work
CHE   Community Home with Education provided on the
           premises. These are run by Social Service Departments
           and used to provide education and care for children in
           care of the local authority, most of whom have have
           committed offences and appeared before the courts.
           CHEs are the successors to the Approved Schools,
           which were run by the Home Office.
CQSW   Certificate of Qualification in Social Work
CSS   Certificate in Social Service
DES   Department of Education and Science
DHSS   Department of Health and Social Security
EBD   Educational and Behavioural Disorders
ESN(M)   Educationally Subnormal (Moderate) (pre-1981
           Education Act category). Now generally replaced by the
           phrase 'children who have moderate learning
           difficulties'. The phrase 'slow learner' is also still quite
           commonly used.
ESN(S)   Educationally Subnormal (Severe). Now replaced by
           'children who have severe learning difficulties'. Often
           associated with the description 'mentally handicapped'.

ILEA	Inner London Education Authority
IT	Intermediate Treatment
LEA	Local Education Authority
Maladjusted	pre-1981 Education Act Category. Description still much used, but replaced in DES lists, etc., by the phrase 'children with emotional and behavioural disorders'. This is shortened in the 1985 Fish Report to the new label 'EBD'.
NAHT	National Association of Headteachers
RSW	Residential Social Worker. Chosen in preference to child-care worker, a term which is used in the text to include both teacher and RSW involved with child-care duties. An alternative term is 'houseparent'. This is now declining in popularity, and is sometimes disliked as it suggests the RSW might be seeking to be a 'parent' in place of the child's natural mother and father. Another possible alternative, the term 'group worker', is felt by the author to be impersonal and misleading, in that it does not allow for the one-to-one work with pupils for which the RSW should, on occasion, have time.

1

Life in the Dinosaurs

BOARDERS PAST AND PRESENT

Jenny was a timid blind girl with no additional social or educational difficulties who lived with her stable parents in a comfortable house in a remote rural town. It was not considered possible to educate her at the local primary school so her mother and father, with many misgivings and feelings of guilt, accepted that she must go to residential school 200 miles away. When she reached secondary age, she transferred to a school ninety miles from home. Unlike most of the other children she was never able to go home at weekends.

Cathy had very little hearing. As a four-year-old at a special pre-school unit, her teacher reported an increasingly silent and lethargic child who was frequently short of sleep, seemed physically neglected, and showed no signs of becoming toilet trained. While disputing the alleged inadequate caring, her parents agreed reluctantly that she should go, at the age of five, to a residential school for the hearing impaired.[1]

Angie has cerebral palsy and spends most of her waking hours in a wheelchair. As an adult, she looks back with displeasure at the residential school she entered at the age of six. In those days, boarding placement seemed the natural response to her special needs.[2]

Sean's mother did little for her son. He had to find food for himself and spent much of his time roaming the streets of a large Northern city. Truancy and petty pilfering led to his being taken into the care of the local authority and, at the age of nine, placed in a boarding school. In the holidays, he indulged in increasing criminal activity leading to police involvement. As he grew older, he took to joy-riding in cars. When once more he ran away and stole a car, the school asked for his transfer. A spell at Detention Centre followed the resulting court appearance. He then entered a Community Home with Education provided on the premises. By this time he was well and truly set on a delinquent career.

Janet was a frail nine-year-old when admitted to a mixed junior boarding school for the maladjusted on the outskirts of her town. At home, her sometimes bizarre behaviour had included killing her pet rabbit and defecating in her bedroom. At day school she had made little progress in reading and number, and had been unhappy, fretful and listless. In class, she was quietly disruptive and destructive. If reprimanded she would react violently, flailing her arms and loudly protesting her innocence. This she would sometimes follow with acts of self-mutilation — picking continuously at scabs on her wrist, or even cutting herself with a knife. Baffled by her behaviour, parents and day-school staff were pleased for her to experience the alternative educational and social lifestyle of a 'therapeutic community'.

Darren's father had a drink problem and had served prison sentences for repeated minor offences. His mother could not easily cope with her lively son's naughty behaviour, and his day school found him disruptive. His parents then parted. His social worker and educational psychologist agreed that residential placement for the ten-year-old boy in a school which specialised in helping children with learning difficulties would 'prop up' the family situation and best meet Darren's educational needs.

Alex had caring parents who had grown to be very suspicious of anybody representing 'authority'. They did not believe it was their son's fault when he was suspended from comprehensive school at the age of fourteen for serious aggressive and rude behaviour towards the staff and other pupils. They similarly found it hard to accept that he was involved in delinquent behaviour around the neighbourhood, but were happy that he should be given a fresh start at a residential school for children with emotional and behavioural difficulties.

Paul was a timid and withdrawn eleven-year-old who suffered from epilepsy, although this was controlled by drugs. His well-to-do parents recognised that they were over-protective towards their son. They did not want him to attend the local day school for children with moderate learning difficulties or the local authority's own boarding school for epileptics. They pressed for him to be placed in an independent residential special school. Eventually the local authority agreed to their request.

WHO SHOULD BOARD?

These brief sketches illustrate the wide variety of children attending residential special schools and their differing family circumstances.

Further contrasting examples could have been given — for example, the mentally handicapped child with severe behavioural problems in a residential school who would otherwise have lived in a subnormality hospital; or the highly intelligent but disturbed and suicidal teenager studying in boarding school for university entrance. But whatever the differences in their case histories, boarders can be divided into two groups: a numerically small and shrinking group with physical or sensory impairments, and a much larger group with serious behavioural, family or other social difficulties.

For those children in the first group, of whom Jenny and Angie were examples, no suitable local day special provision is available and both LEA officials and parents accept that these youngsters' educational needs cannot be met in ordinary day schools. These children are likely to attend well-resourced regional centres of expertise generously staffed and specially adapted to their particular needs. For such children, the residential side of boarding-school life is a necessary but definitely subservient feature. They attend the school primarily for *educational* and, in the case of some physically impaired children, for *medical* reasons. Whenever possible pupils only spend four nights on site each week and they do this for the obvious reason that it is too far for them to travel home every night to their families. Their physical or sensory impairments are not compounded by the difficulties which characterise the second group of children, some of whom attend the same special boarding schools as the first group.

For the majority of boarders, providing a suitable education is not necessarily the primary reason for their placement in residential special schools.

The proliferation of day special schools, units and classes over the last quarter century for the children labelled, under the pre-1981 Education Act categories, educationally subnormal (ESN) has brought special provision within easy reach of nearly all such pupils' homes. Gone are the days when the slow-learning child, like the sensory impaired, had to board to receive suitable teaching. At times this could be taken to ridiculous extremes: take as an example the Cornish twins who in the 1960s went to a boarding school situated within fifty miles of the Scottish border. Nowadays, for a child with moderate learning difficulties to be in boarding school, he[3] is likely to have posed quite severe 'acting out' or withdrawn and neurotic behaviour in his day school. But this in itself will not usually warrant the expense of residential placement. If his family situation is stable, he will continue to live at home, and perhaps receive alternative day provision, unless, as in the case of Paul, his parents particularly want their child to go to residential school.

In addition to educational and social problems at day school, there are likely to be severe difficulties in the boarder's home situation. For example, a single parent might find it hard to cope with her son's behaviour, as in the case of Darren. Where a child lives away from his natural family, foster parents or children's home staff may be overtaxed if a disturbed child in their care attends day school and lives with them throughout the year but can manage to cope with him during his holidays from boarding school (see the case of Tommy on p. 34 below). Sometimes the roots of the boarder's difficulties seem to lie in the parents' behaviour, as in the case of Sean, rather than in the child's problems. Occasionally, the difficulties presented by his siblings — perhaps the severe handicap of a sister — may cause a child to board.

Increasingly the same applies to children with physical or sensory impairments. As integration programmes have proceeded or special day provision has been expanded, so the need to board has lessened *except* where children with these impairments also exhibit behaviour problems at school and/or come from stressful or inadequate home circumstances, as in the case of five-year-old Cathy.

Similarly, if a child is said by teachers and psychologist to have emotional and behavioural disorders (the term used since the 1981 Education Act by the Department of Education and Science to describe children previously designated 'maladjusted') he will usually only board if he presents problems at home and school. To be 'maladjusted' at school, but not at home, might justify alternative day provision, but not boarding education, except in rare circumstances. If parents are asked to support residential placement for their child and the latter does not pose severe problems in the family home, the parents are likely to object to this. They might fairly ask whether the child is to go to boarding school for his own benefit, or merely to rid an ordinary secondary school or a day special unit of a member who has become awkward and disruptive largely because the staff have failed to meet his needs. Might not the day establishment have tried harder to adapt curriculum and organisation to prevent the crisis which precipitated the pressure for residential placement?

Such parents' right of veto will not be available to the families of children who have been taken into the care of the local authority. Many of these will have been before the juvenile courts. Until the 1969 Children and Young Persons' Act, placement in residential care and education in the guise of Approved Schools mainly administered by the Home Office, or their successors, after the Act, the Community Homes with Education provided on the premises (CHEs) run by local social services departments, was almost a standard response. As concern has grown at the high rate of recidivism among leavers and the costs of maintaining these establishments have increased substantially, so the use of CHEs has fallen dramatically. The stated aim was always the rehabilitation of the child but placement in these establishments was often viewed as a form of punishment by the youngster involved. It was probably seen in the same light by the members of the child's local community. Such schools isolated and contained children in a generally humane but basically custodial environment. These functions were probably more important than the education provided.

OFFICIAL VIEWS OF BOARDING NEED

Major reports and surveys of the last twenty years have seen a continuing role for residential special education and the descriptions of boarding need contained within them tie in with the ideas introduced above. All point to the twin functions of boarding schools — attacking children's school-related difficulties but also helping to meet family-based needs.

The 1978 Warnock Report gave a broad definition of need, although it did not include the small number of children, usually from rural areas, for whom no suitable local provision is available. It suggested that boarding would

> continue to be needed in the following circumstances which call for a co-ordinated approach to a child's learning and living:
> (i) where a child with severe or complex disabilities requires a combination of medical treatment, therapy, education and care which it would be beyond the combined resources of a day special school and his family to provide, but which does not call for his admission to hospital;
> (ii) where learning difficulties or other barriers to educational progress are so severe that the whole life of the child needs to be under consistent and continuous educational influence, for example where a child is suffering severe sensory loss, extensive neurological damage or malfunction, severe emotional or behavioural disorder or severe difficulties of communication;
> (iii) where a child has a severe disability and his parents cannot provide at home the sustained attention that he needs, or could not do so without unacceptable consequences for family life and the well-being of the other children in the family;
> (iv) where poor social conditions or disturbed family relationships either contribute or exacerbate the child's educational difficulty.[4]

Among the children encompassed by this are the most numerous group of boarders, the children with emotional and behavioural disorders. In 1965, Inner London Education Authority psychiatrists suggested that residential education could help such children when

- a child was becoming delinquent or was at risk in other ways in the community;
- the child's parents were unable to control the child adequately;

- parental attitudes were considered to be so unfavourable that they were unlikely to be modified;
- the child was from a broken home.[5]

Robert Laslett was also concerned with the maladjusted. He reported a survey, conducted in 1970, for which the staff of more than a hundred child guidance clinics were asked to identify the criteria they used to justify a child's placement in a special boarding school. Their answers included both school-based and home-based factors. The psychiatrists and psychologists of twenty six clinics suggested 'school unable to manage or has excluded child' and a further sixteen 'breakdown in school or child unable to manage at school'. But their replies more commonly referred to difficulties in the family home. Amongst these were 'breakdown in relationships at home', 'parents attitudes not modifiable in short term', 'removal of child necessary for child and family', and 'the child cannot improve while remaining at home'. Only six clinics thought school factors alone justified residential placement and of these, three had no local day school for the maladjusted.

The social work function of residential education is also made apparent in Ewan Anderson's 1978 survey of attitudes of LEA staff towards supporting the placement of children in maintained boarding schools. While not special schools, these establishments do admit many pupils with social needs. The survey does give a useful insight into education officials' thinking. All LEAs were asked if they would be prepared to consider support for boarding if a child had needs which fell into one of a list of categories. Over three-quarters of LEAs said they would support boarding if there were severe family problems, perhaps springing from divorce, handicap or illness, criminal behaviour or if a child was in moral danger or did not receive adequate care.[7]

Most recently the 1985 ILEA-sponsored Fish Report, which favoured the extension of integrated education to as many pupils as possible, recognised a continuing role for residential special schools. Criteria suggested for the placement of children with emotional and behavioural difficulties overlap extensively with those given in the preceding paragraphs. They add that boarding can best meet the special needs of children with parents whose jobs mean that they have to move location frequently, interrupting a child's day schooling. Importantly they also recognise that parents may *choose* boarding placement,[8] a right which Paul's parents (see p. 2) found difficult to exercise.

In the light of this opinion it is not surprising that an extensive though admittedly shrinking national system of special boarding schools continues to exist.

THE RANGE OF PROVISION

To give an exact picture of national provision is difficult. DES Statistics of Education are the best source,[9] but changes in methods of collection and in definitions make it impossible to chart trends with precision. Further, certain useful facts are not included, for example no breakdown is published of the numbers of boarders and day pupils placed by LEAs in the 100 or so independent residential special schools approved by the DES. Similarly, the basic problem of the precise definition of a boarding school has to be examined. Until 1984, the DES defined as a boarding school any school providing residential provision for five or more pupils. For many years, this helped to hide the decline of the popularity of boarding. The statistics now divide schools into 'mainly boarding' and 'mainly day', although this too can be misleading, and might lead observers to overlook over 2,300 boarders in 'mainly day' schools in 1984. Another useful source of information, the *Education Authorities Directory*,[10] also has limitations. In particular it does not divide private independent schools (often run as partnerships or limited companies) from the non-maintained (generally schools run by charities and eligible for some central government help). Both are merely described as 'voluntary schools'.

With these caveats in mind, in 1984 there were about 490 special schools in England providing boarding facilities. In addition, there were forty in Scotland, thirty in Wales and ten in Northern Ireland. To these might be added (from a fast shrinking sector) about 100 CHEs run by social services departments. This gives a total of over 650 establishments which might be classified as residential schools. Figure 1 shows the numbers in 1983 of English and Welsh maintained and non-maintained special schools making boarding provision split into broad handicap groupings, based upon categories of handicap spawned by the 1944 Education Act. This was the last year in which these categories were used. However the figure for 'mainly boarding' schools is likely to be under 500, of which, in England and Wales, in January 1984, 202 were 'maintained' (run by local education authorities) and 85 were 'non-maintained'.

At the beginning of 1984 there were approximately 21,000 full-time boarders in English and Welsh maintained, non-maintained and independent special schools or about 16 per cent of the total special school population. Over two-thirds were boys. There is a mixture of coeducational and single-sex establishments. According to DES statistics, 36 per cent of the children experienced a curriculum which closely ressembled that provided in mainstream day schools. Reflecting a definite trend for special boarding schools to be used increasingly for children with

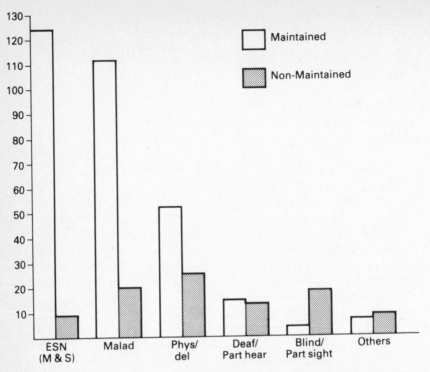

Figure 1. Number of Maintained and Non-Maintained Special Schools Making Boarding Provision, 1983 (England and Wales)

learning difficulties, often in addition to other handicaps, 46 per cent received a 'modified' and 18 per cent a 'developmental' curriculum, similar to those provided in day schools for children with intellectual impairments.

Splitting types of boarding school according to kinds of curriculum reflected the abolition of the old categories originally introduced by the 1944 Education Act. In the 1983 DES statistics these had grown into no less than nineteen. Many boarders would span two or more handicap divisions. Details are given in the Appendix (Table 1), where it will be seen that 88 per cent of the blind educated in maintained and non-maintained English and Welsh special schools, 54 per cent of the deaf, 47 per cent of the maladjusted, 18 per cent of the physically handicapped and 9 per cent of the ESN(M) were residential pupils. In Figure 2, many of the categories have been combined. Following this simplified method of analysis, approximately 35 per cent of boarders in special schools show emotional and behavioural difficulties but fall in the normal range of intelligence; 30 per cent have moderate learning difficulties

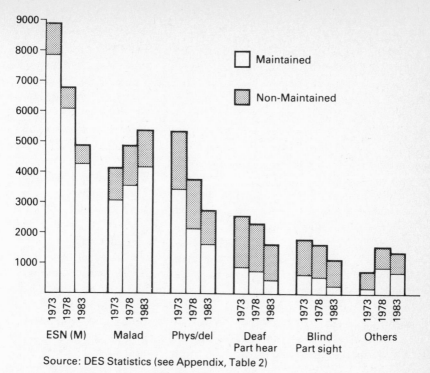

Source: DES Statistics (see Appendix, Table 2)

Figure 2. Number of Full-Time Boarders in Maintained and Non-Maintained Residential Special Schools, 1973, 1978 and 1983 (England and Wales)

of which most show disturbed behaviour; 15 per cent are physically handicapped or delicate and 15 per cent have sensory impairments. Pupils who are epileptic, autistic, have severe speech defects or severe learning difficulties make up the remaining 5 per cent.

Figure 2 (see also Table 2 in the Appendix) shows clear trends in provision over the last decade. For most groups there has been definite movement away from the residential approach. The number of boarders in maintained and non-maintained English and Welsh schools declined between 1973 and 1983 as follows: ESN(M) by about 44 per cent; phsyically handicapped and delicate, 50 per cent; deaf and partially hearing, 38 per cent; blind and partially sighted, 35 per cent. These figures might in part be explained by the fall in population but they also reflect the growth of day alternatives. For example, between 1971 and 1977 day units for the partially hearing increased from 212 to 463.[11] There has also been a greater willingness on the part of local authorities, probably in response to parental pressures, to provide daily transport to schools as far as fifty miles from the child's home. Motorway developments have helped to make this possible. To a lesser extent, though not apparent in the 1982 DES statistics[12] or 1985 Fish Report,[13] the advance of integration may also be contributing to the decline.

In contrast, over the same decade, the numbers of maladjusted in residential education has expanded by 31 per cent in maintained and non-maintained schools, and probably by a quarter in independent schools. There has also been a dramatic percentage increase, although numerically very small, in the number of boarding pupils with speech defects and severe learning difficulties.

Figure 3 (see also Table 3 in the Appendix) shows the expansion and then decline in the number of boarders. A peak was reached in 1975. It also demonstrates the growth in the number of children placed by local education authorities in independent schools. Most of these will be boarders. The growth in this practice has now levelled off.

Geographically, provision is very uneven. In 1984 Dorset (population 0.6 million) had only one school making residential provision, while Lincolnshire (with about the same population) had eight. In the same year the London boroughs (population 4.4 million) had a mere seven residential special schools while Derbyshire (population 0.9 million) had ten. There were seven special schools making boarding provision in South Yorkshire; six of these were in Sheffield and none in Barnsley or Rotherham. Reflecting the tendency for independent schools to be founded in attractive countryside, there was only one voluntary boarding school within the ILEA area while seventeen existed in Devon. Provision in Scotland is sparse and almost half the schools (other than List D schools for young offenders) are run by voluntary bodies.

Most boarding schools are situated in the countryside, small rural towns or by the seaside, usually many miles from their pupils' homes. Of thirty-one ILEA special boarding schools, twenty-four are situated in the Home Counties or on the south coast. This situation resulted from both the preferences and the pragmatism of pioneers and early planners. In Victorian times escape to arcadia for the children of Mary Carpenter's 'dangerous and perishing classes',[14] away from cholera epidemics and the twilight criminal existence of Dickens's Artful Dodger, seemed many children's likeliest salvation. In this century, sea breezes or fresh country air have been chosen in preference to city smog for the delicate (asthmatics, children with brittle bones, weak hearts, etc.) and physically handicapped.

Further, in the wake of the 1944 Education Act, local authorities, unable to afford or lacking time to design and build new schools on town sites, followed central government advice[15] in buying the country mansions of impecunious gentry at discount prices and converting them into boarding schools. This was a quick and pragmatic way of responding to

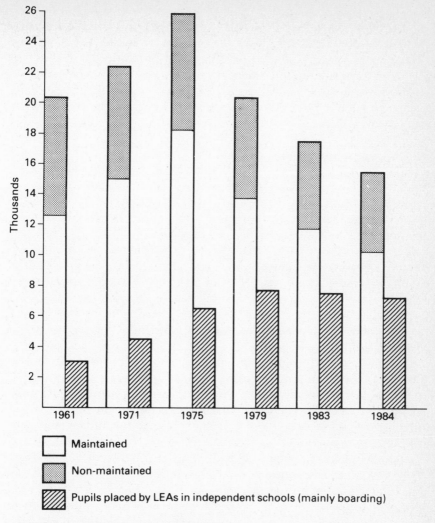

Source: DES *Statistics of Education*

Figure 3. Number of Boarders in Maintained and Non-Maintained Schools and Number of Handicapped Pupils Placed in Independent Special Schools

the Act's demands that suitable provision be made for the new official categories of handicapped children — particularly the increasing numbers labelled ESN or maladjusted.

Some local authorities with little provision of their own have been content to use the non-maintained and independent sectors. Others, particularly the metropolitan boroughs, for example those circling

Manchester and Liverpool, created by local government reorganisation in 1974, were forced to do the same. Still others have always preferred to meet special needs using non-residential approaches. These are now being joined by LEAs who have changed tack in recent years. As an example of the latter, Manchester Metropolitan District has closed down two residential schools for ESN(M) children, one for epileptics and one for the physically handicapped which it used to maintain in neighbouring rural Cheshire.

LIFE IN THE DINOSAURS

Education officers and psychologists working in LEAs not favouring the residential approach might be strongly influenced by the high cost of providing residential education. They may also have succeeded in integrating most of their physically and sensory handicapped children. Further, they may be influenced by advocates of a *preventive* rather than a *curative* approach to disaffected youngsters with special needs, some of whom at present enter segregated boarding provision.

David Galloway and other authors[16] argue strongly that the efforts of professionals should be applied to identifying and rectifying the way a substantial minority of children in ordinary schools are alienated from the school system. It is claimed that perhaps a fifth of secondary pupils feel that the curriculum has little relevance for them and believe that they have been labelled failures. Among these are the tiny minority who are transferred to day and residential special schools. Rather than spend heavily on these schools, these writers argue that it would be more sensible and more helpful to a greater number of children to put the limited resources available into advising and training front-line teachers to meet more effectively the needs of the less able and disaffected. They also recommend altering the curriculum and organisation so that an ethos is created in *ordinary* day schools which welcomes and encourages these youngsters and gives them the chance to succeed in a range of activities which boosts their feelings of self-esteem. They point out that some schools achieve this already, and consequently refer less children to segregated provision. If the ethos of these successful schools could be replicated in the less successful, then the need to segregate children would be greatly diminished.

Such an approach, if more widely translated into effective practice would undoubtedly make many day special schools redundant and perhaps some residential special schools which have been used incorrectly as dumping grounds for the rejects of secondary schools.

However there would remain the children with special educational needs and home/social difficulties. While a tiny number in comparison to the total national school population, they still run into some thousands. That such children exist has been established on an empirical basis by various studies which have found that difficult behaviour at home is significantly associated with poor academic performance and behavioural problems at school.[17]

At present residential special education performs a useful role in helping these children. The following chapter looks in some depth at how boarding schools might be relieved of this function. In it are described social work approaches which can bring relief to families under stress and substitute carers responsible for a child with special educational needs. If social services departments and the major voluntary child-care agencies could make these effective and popular with children and their families on a *national* scale, many children at present in residential education would no longer need to board.

With improved ethos in most secondary schools and effective home-based social work alternatives, the days of most residential schools would clearly be numbered. Anticipating this situation, the head of a semi-integrated special unit attached to a comprehensive school recently described residential special schools as the 'dinosaurs of the education system'.[18] However, if the practical difficulties of making the necessary changes are considered, such a description seems premature. In the present imperfect world, where lack of resources and the inertia of established practice block innovation and improvements in day schools, residential special education would still seem to have a role to play for some years to come. The ensuing chapters are written on the assumption that this prognosis is correct, and that it is worth working for the improvement of a service which, although slimmed down, is going to continue to be needed. What then, are the aims of the book?

It sometimes appears as though a thick oak door divides the residential special school from the outside world. Teachers and residential social workers (RSWs) behind the door have not the time or sometimes lack the inclination to open it to concerned professionals and parents of prospective and actual pupils to show them the excellent practice which in the best schools has been developed. Meanwhile, the shut door muffles the sounds of innovatory practices evolving in the day schools and the children's home communities, some of which could be usefully copied by isolated boarding schools. In this door there may be a small window — a darkened whorl of ancient glass, distorting both the perceptions of those looking out and those wishing to look in.

Those outside may form their impressions of residential education from occasional scandals in the newspapers, or from research into particular forms of boarding schools (for example, the old Approved Schools) which are not representative of a broad and varied field. The good work of staff and the happiness and progress of many boarders who had previously had a dismal experience of education in unsuitable day schools may be overlooked.

Meanwhile, teachers and RSWs behind the thick door may have been sucked into the vortex of emotions, conflicts, stressful relationships, and tiring duties which can characterise some boarding schools and which leave them with little energy or desire to find out what is happening in the world outside. Others may have relapsed into a soporific state in a cocooned rural community, providing adequate care and a basic education for the pupils, but knowing less and less about the harsh realities of the children's home lives and their depressed urban neighbourhoods. In these sometimes unreal sanctuaries, staff can develop an inward-looking attitude to their work, failing to check the relevance of their approach in a changing world.

This book seeks to open the door a little, to give an impression of special boarding life to professionals and concerned parents, pointing to the features which will be present in the well-organised and effective schools. At the same time it is hoped to provoke thought in those working within these schools, to prompt them to examine the day-to-day practice of their own establishment, to think about major relevant approaches with which they may not be familiar, and from which ideas may be usefully borrowed. Organisations have a habit of becoming orientated to the needs of those who work in them and away from the needs of those they serve. This tendency has been noted in some research relating to one form of special boarding education.[19] Teachers and residential care workers are asked to identify areas in their own schools which could be improved the better to meet the special needs of the children and their families.

First however, they are asked to think further of special boarding's *raison d'être*. It has already been stated that the social work as much as the educational function of a boarding school may lead to a child being placed there. Perhaps too little thought is given by residential workers to alternative methods of relieving the stresses of some family homes by means which do not require the child to live away from his family and do allow him to remain in day school and part of his local community, in other words avoiding the common criticism that residential schooling severs a child from his natural roots. Chapter 2 seeks to challenge the complacent attitude sometimes heard in boarding school staffrooms: 'There may be less children around, but there will always be plenty of our sort of pupil.' Those who think in this way ought to consider the various social work approaches which have developed and expanded in recent years and which, if made effective on a national scale, could threaten the continued existence of many special boarding schools. However, more reassuringly to those employed in boarding schools, the goal of national effectiveness for these family-based 'community care' approaches remains distant and it is argued that even in the long term there will still be a few children better served by special boarding.

The opening pages of this chapter gave an indication of the wide variety of children at present in boarding, but not of the contrasting forms of organisation or the conflicting theories which different schools adopt. It is hoped that Chapter 3 will widen the knowledge of both the concerned 'outsider' and also the cocooned 'insider' whose work commitment does not allow him to visit differing schools, or to study the common theories underpinning residential practice. Lack of training opportunities can too commonly lead to this situation, leaving personal experience and the traditions of his own particular school as the only benchmarks against which the worker can measure his own and his school's performance.

In Chapter 4, discussion turns to the components of good daily practice in boarding schools. First the overlap between the goals of 'education' and 'care' is stressed. It is regretted that in some boarding schools a strict and harmful departmentalism can exist. Teachers work the day shift. Residential social workers work the unsocial hours and there is little communication between the two, although they are often working towards the same ends, particularly in the children's social and 'life skills' education. A plea is made for the extension of 'integrated timetabling' whereby teachers play some part in the evening lives of the children and RSWs help in some daytime class activities. This seems the best way of tackling the lack of co-operation and understanding between different professions which blights too many boarding schools. Following from this, Chapter 5, on the components of sound educational curriculum, is the concern of the RSW, while Chapter 6, on what constitutes good child care, should be studied by the teacher.

The width of educational experience offered to many special school pupils is, in theory at least, narrower than that offered to pupils in ordinary schools, where much greater numbers on roll and consequently more resources make the provision of a wide subject choice easier. Despite high staff–pupil ratios, even the large residential special school with well over 100 pupils finds it hard to compete in this respect. Boarding schools must therefore compensate by providing a carefully planned and well-implemented curriculum, closely geared to the individual needs of its pupils. 'Containing' difficult children in class is no longer sufficient justification for the high cost of residential placement. Chapter 5 sketches some of the major educational considerations which will already be familiar to curriculum planners but may not be known by new residential workers or parents wishing to assess the quality of a school.

Similarly, it is inadequate for children merely to be fed and 'warehoused' in moderate comfort between the end of afternoon lessons and the beginning of lessons next morning. Even worse, and perhaps still existing in a few schools, is an institutionalising approach to child care which denies the existence of pupils' emotional needs, provides them with a lifestyle far inferior to that enjoyed by a child living with his natural or foster family and leaves them ill prepared for life when they leave school. Chapter 6 indicates the basic ingredients of good child care.

Chapter 7 seeks to widen the picture of boarding life for 'outsiders', by sketching what it can be like to work in a residential school. It also prompts residential workers to look at the organisation of their own school, and its provision for staff support, relaxation and training. For the community to be vibrant and the employees alive to the needs of the children, these are important issues. The quality of the educational and caring experience provided for the pupils is likely to reflect the well-being and motivation of the staff.

Teachers are said to be poor at cultivating and maintaining good relations with parents.[20] This tendency can be worsened if the school is eighty miles from the family home and there is little contact between the two. So, thinking of the need for boarding-school staff to do all they can to mitigate the effects of splitting a child from his family and his community, Chapter 8 urges that a continuing effort is made during a child's stay in residential school to keep parents involved in their children's education. Only with their backing and support can the residential experience significantly benefit the child.

The final chapter looks to the future and gives some samples of consumer opinion on the value of boarding.

Throughout the book most attention is given to children with emotional, behavioural and learning difficulties. This is a conscious decision, in part reflecting the constraints placed upon the length of this book, but also the predominance of these difficulties in the majority of children at present in special boarding schools no matter what the official description of their school. Figure 1 showed that in 1983 there were more boarding schools for the maladjusted than for any other category. Children with moderate learning difficulties generally board for social, emotional and behavioural reasons. Further, figures given by various authors[21] suggest that between a third and a half of the children in schools for the physically and sensory impaired also have learning difficulties. Many of these children also display emotional and behavioural disorders. Thus, teachers and residential social workers in the vast majority of residential schools will be concerned with disturbed children with some degree of learning difficulty.

NOTES

1. J. Statham, 'Routes to a Residential School for the Deaf' in T. Booth and J. Statham (eds), *The Nature of Special Education*, Croom Helm in association with the Open University Press, London, 1982, pp. 50–3.
2. J. Campling, *Images of Ourselves*, Routledge and Kegan Paul, London, 1981, pp. 8–12.
3. Throughout this book, use of 'he' implies 'he or she'.
4. Committee of Enquiry into the Education of Handicapped Children and Young People, *Special Educational Needs* (Warnock Report), Cmnd. 7212, HMSO, London, 1978, para. 8.16, p. 126.
5. M.C. Roe, *Survey into Progress of Maladjusted Pupils*, ILEA, London, 1965.
6. R. Laslett, *Educating Maladjusted Children*, Granada, London, 1977, p. 63.
7. E.W. Anderson, Research Topics no. 4, Boarding Schools Association, 1980.
8. Committee Reviewing Provision to Meet Special Educational Needs, *Educational Opportunities for All* (Fish Report), ILEA, London, 1985, para. 2.9.59, p. 95.
9. Figures 1, 2 and 3 are based on DES *Statistics of Education*. Because of varying methods of collection, exact figures cannot be given nor precise comparisons made between one table and another or one year and another.
10. *Education Authorities Directory*, School Government Publishing Company, Redhill, 1984.
11. M. Nolan and I. Tucker, *The Hearing Impaired Child and His Family*, Souvenir Press, London, 1981, p. 198.
12. See W. Swann, 'Statistics of Segregation', *Childright*, Children's Legal Centre, June 1984, pp. 18–19.
13. Fish Report, para. 1.4.21, p. 25.
14. M. Carpenter, *Reformatory Schools for the Children of the Dangerous and Perishing Classes and for Juvenile Offenders*, Gilpin, London, 1851.
15. Ministry of Education, *Boarding School Provision for Educationally Sub-Normal and Maladjusted Children*, Circular 79, HMSO, London, 1946.
16. D. Galloway, 'Institutional Change or Individual Change? An Overview' in B. Gillham, *Problem Behaviour in the Secondary School*, Croom Helm, London, 1981; D. Galloway and C. Goodwin, *Educating Slow Learning Children: Integration or Segregation*, Longman, London, 1979; see also A. Skinner, A. Platts and B. Hall, *Disaffection from School: Issues and Interagency Responses*, National Youth Bureau, Leicester, 1983.
17. See S. Mitchell and M. Shepherd, 'A Comparative Study of Children's Behaviour at Home and at School', *British Journal of Educational Psychology*, vol. 36, pp. 248–54.
18. Personal communication.
19. Schools allowing 'organisational' rather than 'instrumental' and 'affective' goals to predominate, described in S. Millham, R. Bullock and P. Cherrett, *After Grace, Teeth*, Chaucer, London, 1975.
20. For example, Galloway and Goodwin, *Educating Slow Learning Children*, p. 138.

21. E.M. Anderson, L. Clarke and B. Spain, *Disability in Adolescence*, Methuen, London, 1982, p. xv; A.H. Bowley and L. Gardner, *The Handicapped Child*, Churchill Livingstone, Edinburgh, 1980, p. 192; K.P. Meadow, *Deafness and Child Development*, Arnold, London, 1980.

2

Social Work Alternatives to Special Boarding and their Limitations

The Warnock Report notes that some parents of children with special needs 'have burdens to bear of which other people may have no conception'. [1] These 'other people' might include professionals who mistakenly steer parents away from the residential approach even though these families are 'intolerably overtaxed',[2] inducing in them guilt feelings for even considering the idea. So first a reminder is given of the intense stresses born by some parents.

PRESSURES ON THE FAMILY

'A handicapped child can mean a handicapped home' suggested the National Union of Teachers in its evidence to the Warnock Committee. The special care required by a child with a physical disability and no additional problems can be time-consuming, exhausting and severely disrupt normal living even for the most resilient family. Dressing, undressing and feeding the child may be major tasks. Toileting a child or managing the accidents of the incontinent may be regular daily jobs. Trying to develop the youngster's ability to perform these functions for himself is likely to be a long, problematic task, stretching over many years. The temptation will always be there to do everything for the child to save time or to avoid argument. The parents' fatigue will be further increased if, for example, sleep is interrupted each night because a parent has to turn a physically handicapped child over in his bed at regular intervals. Pressure will be further increased if much time has to be spent on awkward journeys on public transport to and from hosptial clinics for check-ups and therapy.

An already stressful situation will be made worse if the child has a secondary disability or is multi-handicapped. As has already been emphasised, many hearing impaired and visually impaired as well as physically handicapped children have learning difficulties. Some have sensory, physical *and* intellectual impairments. Further worry and disruption, and possibly loss of parental control, may also be caused by tantrums and other 'acting out' behaviour.

As an extreme example of the stress caused by a multi-handicapped child, take the case of Emma, a mentally handicapped girl whose bizarre behaviour was endured for eight years before effective help was found:

> She would not go to bed before her parents and elder sister, and once everyone was settled she would start a type of musical beds which continued throughout the night. Not only did Emma change places: by means of grunts and gestures she directed her family on a nocturnal merry-go-round ... Emma tended to settle for only ten or fifteen minutes between moves.[3]

During the daytime she would sometimes ensure she got her own way by vomiting, urinating or defecating in the family living room or whichever room she was in. Usually the threat of these actions was sufficient to force her parents to surrender to her wishes.

Mothers and fathers of difficult able-bodied children as well as those with physical impairments may be frightened to leave their house and cannot ask friends or grandparents to 'babysit'. Holidays can be unhappy experiences best avoided. Fathers and mothers sometimes have to give up good jobs to devote more time to the child, resulting in low family income. Meanwhile the needs of the other non-handicapped children in the family might be neglected, increasing parents' anxiety and guilt feelings. Despite anxiously 'keeping up appearances' and not overtly breaking down, these families are scarcely coping.[4]

Problems caused by the child's difficulties might be exacerbated by other forms of stress. The stable family unit may be threatened by one or both parents' ill health, or problems with a child's brothers or sisters. Quite commonly, children in residential special education come from one-parent families or the lives of their close relatives are punctuated with marital problems, acrimonious divorces, strained relationships with cohabitants, financial troubles, and other difficult situations.

Such family stresses amplify the child's own difficulties. He might react with more awkward behaviour within the home. Some able-bodied but maladjusted children also become involved in vandalism or other forms of delinquency around the neighbourhood. Trouble can result between the family and their neighbours because of a child's actions. This sometimes leads to an unfortunate cycle of the family scapegoating and intermittently rejecting the child, who responds with further testing behaviour. Family and child find it difficult to escape from unhelpful stereotyped responses. Assistance is urgently needed by parent and child to help them adjust their attitudes to one another, perhaps to help reawaken a dormant mutual affection.

A RESIDENTIAL OR HOME-BASED RESPONSE TO FAMILY STRESS?

Whatever the difficulties, natural bonds of affection will make nearly every family want to keep their child at home. They might also share the concerns of Nicola Schaeffer, a mother of a severely mentally handicapped child:

> All parents, including myself of course, are defensive about the awful decision of whether to keep or institutionalize a handicapped child. I didn't realise at the time that many people who do take the latter course are faced with the accusation, sometimes veiled but often viciously explicit, that they don't love their child.[5]

While allowing one's child to attend a residential school during term times only, with weekends at home, does not equal placing one's child in a large subnormality hospital, possibly for life — the only alternative available to Nicola Schaeffer — the worry and guilt can still be intense. So, instead of the common response of residential care in a children's home or boarding school, what else can be done to help the child and to ease the family burden?

In the last thirty years various forms of help have been developed and expanded, although in somewhat patchy fashion, which allow the child to remain in his own home and neighbourhood. These range from traditional social work counselling approaches through to 'Intermediate Treatment' — the name given to a range of programmes of social and educational activities organised by social services and voluntary agencies for children who have been in trouble with the police, have home problems or are at risk in other ways and yet do not require full-time, long-term residential care.

If it is felt necessary for a child to be taken into the care of the local authority and away from the parents, many social workers now prefer to use fostering in preference to placement in a children's home or boarding school. This, it is argued, at least provides a life in a family home with special adults caring for the child, so that he remains part of a local community and attends day school. It can also be cheaper.

Where these approaches work well, the need for special boarding education can be significantly reduced. Unfortunately in practice these responses do not always provide as effective an answer. Shortcomings in organisation or staffing levels have been noted which are not easy to remedy. Further, the children or their families may not react as might have been anticipated to such 'community care'. While some parents passionately oppose residential placement, others put pressure upon reluctant professionals to support their child in residential school. Finally there are a few children in care who have had difficulties in foster and children's homes and find boarding-school life preferable.

Later sections of this chapter will examine these limitations to community-care approaches. But first we examine the range of home- and substitute-home-based responses which avoid boarding. Modes of intervention form a continuum from least to most intensive and expensive. The sections below will follow this pattern.

THE TRADITIONAL SOCIAL WORK APPROACH

The field social worker, whether attached to a child-guidance clinic, school, hospital department or the local authority social services department is likely to be the channel through which assistance is brought to both parent and child in their own home. In liaison with other concerned professionals, he assesses the needs of the household, and then helps the client obtain the required specialist service. He presses for financial assistance to purchase equipment needed to help a family cope better with a physically handicapped child. He urges the local housing department to rectify defects in the fabric of the house which contribute to a family's problems. He can press for alternative accommodation, for example, a downstairs flat. He can speak up for the parents at the child's school.

Intervention on the family's behalf outside the home is likely to accompany counselling of parents on how to solve or alleviate their difficulties using their own resources. When a trusting relationship has been built up, the family may be ready to accept advice on how to reorganise their lives in order better to cope with their child's problems.

Similar advice might be received from health visitor, educational welfare officer or specialists at the child-guidance clinic or hospital unit. The child's teachers might also extend their work in this direction, by visiting the family home and talking to the parents.

For the families of a few children in boarding schools, help along these lines, not at present given, may be sufficient to enable the child to remain at home and attend day school.

FAMILY AND DAY CENTRES

Parents who are reluctant to receive such help in their homes, perhaps fearing the critical attitude of neighbours or opposition from other members of the family, can go to the child-guidance clinic or a 'walk-in' or 'phone-in' advice bureau such as the Family Centre in Sheffield,[6] where various professional advisors are housed in the same building. Parents are encouraged to meet one another, share experiences and offer mutual support.

Assistance goes beyond talk and psychological testing at some day-care centres. It can be argued that it is not possible to alter the behaviour of parent and child in any meaningful way when one is split from the other by residential care. Might not lasting change only be brought about by working simultaneously with child and parent in the same building? Mothers therefore accompany their young child to the centre each day. Staff initially work with the boy or girl to demonstrate the effectiveness of the methods they use. The parent sees the child responding to the staff approaches and becomes more responsive to advice and practical training in child-care skills. Lasting beneficial change can be brought about which eradicates the need for the child to be placed in a childen's home or boarding school.

DIRECT PARENT TRAINING AND PRACTICAL HELP IN THE FAMILY HOME

The Family Rehabilitation Centres run by Hertfordshire social services are an extension of the approach described above. Entire families whose deep-seated problems might be working to the detriment of the children are accommodated at these centres while RSWs and other professional workers advise and instruct parents, developing child-care skills and strategies to deal with stress.

If a person's behaviour is largely a reaction to his physical and emotional environment, offering training to parents actually within their home, where most of their immediate difficulties occcur, would seem a desirable course. Staff from a psychiatric unit in Belfast have practised a policy of teaching simple behaviour-modification techniques to mothers of difficult children with special needs in the family living-room or bathroom.[7] Perhaps more day-school and child-guidance staff should extend their work actually into the family home to ensure transfer of successful methods from the classroom or clinic to the home. Furthermore, the European example of the social pedagogue spending extended periods in the family home, sometimes living with them, could be followed more frequently in this country. It would be helpful if money were to be found to try to copy and evaluate American or Scandinavian 'homemaker' or 'family-aide' schemes.[8] In a five-year Finnish experiment, specialist 'homemakers' were attached to multi-problem families. During the initial settling-in period the 'homemaker' concentrated on domestic activities, relieving the mundane daily pressures on parents. Gradually the approach became more educative, showing parents appropriate methods of child care, suggesting sources of help for particular difficulties, and helping a family obtain this assistance. After five years, despite some difficulties, the scheme has been extended to other areas of the country.

Much of this work would not be of a specialist nature, requiring long professional training, and could fall within the ambit of the Home Help Service, nearly 90 per cent of whose clients are at present the aged.[9] With some expansion of resources, could not more assistance be channelled into the homes of families with a child with special needs? With the burden of housework lightened, and a receptive companion to listen and advise, the overtaxed mother would be given chance to face up to her task of coping with more energy and effectiveness with the difficult handicapped child on his return from day school and during holiday periods. She would be further helped if aid could be provided in the evenings around the child's bedtime, or at weekends when school was not open. Such family aides would be useful whether the child had learning difficulties, was disturbed or had a physical disability.

For the latter there could also be need for special medical assistance from nurses, or Health Service therapists. Were extra resources made available for improved peripatetic or locally based services the excellent facilities of some regionally-based residential special schools might be matched for convenience and effectiveness.

EXTENDING THE 'INTERMEDIATE TREATMENT' APPROACH

Another strategy which can reduce the need for residential education and care is to take the child out of his home for periods outside normal school hours and occupy him in a range of beneficial social and educational activities. While 'Intermediate Treatment' schemes emerged in the late 1960s as an alternative provision for young offenders who had traditionally been sent by magistrates for long-term placement in Approved Schools, similar intervention might be useful for the disturbed child with physical or intellectual disabilities and could relieve stress in their families.

IT programmes take many different forms, varying in intensity and duration. Some simply require a child to attend specialist youth clubs twice a week, run by staff with some experience of children with special needs. Others might append the need for a child to attend weekly discussion or counselling groups. If the expertise of teachers and psychologists is harnessed to the skills of social workers, it is possible to make such sessions highly structured, purposeful affairs geared to the child's individual needs, linking to and extending the child's daytime educational experience. The intensity of the programme could be increased for the child posing more severe difficulties at home by individual work out of normal school hours designed to develop the child's life skills, or outdoor pursuits expeditions designed to give him challenge and adventure and foster the development of self-esteem. Some IT programmes will also require short-term residential courses, lasting a few weeks instead of the few years a child might otherwise spend in residential care.

A lively IT initiative is described by its creator and organiser Professor Bob Holman in his book *Kids at the Door*.[10] Holman doubted the efficacy of residential treatment of young offenders in CHEs. He also saw limits to the effectiveness of traditional field social work, suspecting that too often it was imposed on an unwilling clientele by people not in tune with them. Putting beliefs into practice, he moved house to the edge of a troubled council estate and, funded by a national charity, he set up the Bath Community Child Care Project. By working to gain the parents' support and by providing activities and practical assistance using the parents' suggestions, he sought to reduce the number of children placed in the care of the local authority, to alter attitudes of children prone to delinquency and to provide a fuller social life for local teenagers.

Initially much time was spent knocking on doors, making the acquaintance of the whole family, listening to parents' perceptions of local problems and necessary action. When a relationship and respect developed for the team, locals made frequent visits and phone calls to Holman's house to make youth-club arrangements, discuss family problems and seek advice on practical and emotional difficulties. Despite difficulties in gaining initial acceptance, and the youth club's being seen as a source of vandalism and disturbance in its first year, the team gained the support and respect of many parents and children. The latter benefited from the youth-club activities on the estate and on expeditions. In Holman's view, the three-year project did improve the quality of life on the estate, lessening police involvement and probably preventing the need for some children to enter long-term residential care. Contributory factors to the perceived success were the deep involvement of the workers with the parents as well as the children; continued intervention lasting years and the availability of help outside normal working hours.

Perhaps this scheme could be more widely copied. Effectiveness might be enhanced if such projects could have the full backing and support of local government education and social work departments *working together*, linking evening and weekend work to children's daytime educational programmes.

With a little boldness, it should be possible to employ teachers to work more than the usual school day so that they are able to contribute to schemes such as these. The Warnock Committee bemoaned the short time that some children with special needs came into contact with their teachers.[11] Late starting and early finishing means restricted teaching time which compares unfavourably with the spaciousness of the residential school day where, in the good school, children can be involved in purposeful and contrasting educational and leisure activities which hold their interest from early morning to bedtime. In addition, boarding schools sometimes stay open throughout the standard holidays. In exchange for adequate extra remuneration, teachers are happy to play a part in the evening, weekend and holiday curriculum. If LEAs were to offer Additional Duties Allowances to staff in day schools, it should be possible to organise programmes outside normal day-school hours which would help relieve family stress and perhaps prove a cheaper alternative to the need to place a child in full-time boarding education. Many LEAs already run holiday schools for socially deprived pupils, the gifted, or those with special interests and abilities such as music or drama.

IT and less intense forms of intervention described above, effectively carried out, might be all that is required to help families under moderate and perhaps transitory stress, where the child does not need to be taken into full-time council care. However, this latter course will still be necessary for many. For such children, fostering is likely to be method of implementing this.

FOSTERING AS AN ALTERNATIVE TO RESIDENTIAL EDUCATION

When the quality of care in a local authority children's home or boarding school is low, the attractions of fostering are plain to see. When the standards of residential care and education are good and that of fostering indifferent, the former might well suit some children better. This section will be based on the knowledge that much fostering is of high quality.

Even if the relationship between a child and his natural mother is not as crucial to a child's healthy psychological development as once thought, every child ought at least to have a 'key person' to whom he can turn, or as the American Uri Bronfenbrenner commented: 'Every child needs at least one person who is really crazy about him (or her)'.[12] It is often easier to meet this basic need where a child lives as part of a small family group of perhaps four or five people than in a children's home or residential school where a member of staff is responsible for eight or ten children and only during official working hours. Whereas the foster parent can give a child treats, make him feel especially wanted and valued, in short treat him *partially* in relation to his school friends or the neighbours' children, in the group-living situation, staff have to be fair to every child in their care and dare not venture beyond impartiality. Many children will also appreciate a private bedroom and sharing a comfortable family house with adults who are responsible for them every evening and weekend. There are unlikely to be the formal set of rules which every institution has to have. As long as the relationship between child and the host family is satisfactory, this living situation is likely to be superior to a child's receiving care from a number of professional workers who will often travel to work at the 'home' and exclude the child from their social lives in a way that cannot happen in a family home.

Many children in care who are fostered, do establish emotionally supportive relationships with the family with whom they live. These successful placements might be short-term, when parents of a severely handicapped child are persuaded to take a weekend break or longer holiday under schemes such as the 'Shared Care' plan of Barnardo's working with Birmingham social services. Just the occasional weekend apart might mean the difference between the parent continuing to care for the child in their own home and his admission to residential school.

More placements will be long-term. In many cases, possibly for the first time in his life, a child might feel he has a reliable home base, peopled by trustworthy adults to whom he can turn in times of need. This could be the emotional security he has sought which helps him turn away from anti-social behaviour at day school and around his neighbourhood, of which he might still be a part. For the school leaver, the end of fostering is not likely to coincide with the end of his school career, and so the difficult double discontinuity of leaving school and leaving the security of residential care experienced by the child leaving boarding school is avoided.

Professional fostering is a variant designed for the severely handicapped or disturbed teenager. It has proved successful for some children in both Europe and America. One of the earliest and most publicised schemes in this country was the Kent Family Placement Project. Under this, responsible but often untrained adults were paid a salary of half the cost of placing a child in a residential community for the young offender. Kent social services officers were aware of the high rate of recidivism amongst leavers from both conventional and 'therapeutic' style Approved Schools and their CHE successors, and research which suggested that, while children attending residential schools might absorb desirable behaviours in a new environment, they tended to revert to old habits on return to their homes. Against this background a scheme was devised for families to care for difficult teenage children in their homes. The foster parents were supported by specialist social workers who would also conduct fortnightly meetings for the exchange of information, discussion of problems and as a vehicle for in-service training. In addition, new families would have to contract themselves to participate in special study days.[13]

For some children the scheme worked well. The results encouraged similar projects in Strathclyde, Tyneside and elsewhere. So far, professional fostering schemes have been small in scope but could perhaps be expanded until they do provide an alternative to residential education and care for a significant number of children.

LIMITS TO THE EFFECTIVENESS OF TRADITIONAL FIELD SOCIAL WORK

Discussion now moves on from describing the potential of non-residential approaches which help a child remain with his family or at least in a foster home in his local area and attending day school, to consideration of the shortcomings of these methods *as they are now* and, in an imperfect society, where local government has no funds available for extra staffing or innovation, *as they are likely to be* in the next few years. The present uneven and patchy reality means that placement in a special boarding school can still sometimes be the best practical method of meeting a child's educational and social needs while relieving the intense stresses of his family home. Parents and professionals considering the best course of action for a child and his family should compare the range and quality of options available in his locality with the service provided in the best boarding schools within reasonable reach of their home.

First, parents should ask how effective are the field social workers who play the major part in the delivery of neighbourhood-based alternatives to residential care? Opinion (such as that of Professor Holman quoted below) if not conclusive evidence seems to be growing that, given present circumstances, they find the task hard. Too much is expected of too few in an overstretched and underfinanced branch of local government. It is rare for a council to employ as many as one trained field social worker per 1,000 population. Workers are often not able to devote the time they feel is necessary to individual cases. In the 1970s, through necessity, the best and most experienced tended to be promoted from direct family work to administration, leaving much client contact to young and inexperienced workers, who often transferred quickly from one post to another, making the establishment of helpful, lasting relationships with clients difficult. Perhaps as job opportunities have shrunk so the stability and quality of the service has improved, but the criticisms of Professor Holman are likely to remain pertinent in relation to many children who are candidates for residential education:

> Much as I admire the work of council social workers, I concluded that their preventative actions were limited by several factors. Often they carried large and mixed caseloads which included the elderly, the mentally disordered, the disabled and chronically sick as well as families in need of help. Consequently, they could not concentrate on youngsters who might get into trouble. Further, the size of their caseloads and the areas they covered meant that people could not be seen as regularly or as frequently as was necessary. Most important, social workers tended not to live in the localities where they worked. Even their offices might be some miles from the people most in need of help. It followed that social workers could know closely neither the people nor the neighbourhoods where preventative work was needed.[14]

A study conducted in a large southern town found that social workers were not able to devote much time to 'mendable' families who might have benefited most from their intervention. They could provide little more than a 'casualty' and information service. They could give short-term assistance to tackle a major presenting problem, perhaps referring a family to another agency such as the DHSS, but then had to withdraw through lack of manpower or community facilities:

> In accordance with area policy once they had sorted the immediate crisis and ensured that the family had a roof over their heads, some basic income and their children were not neglected or otherwise at serious risk, they closed the case, often aware that many stresses and problems were still present and remained untouched by their intervention.[15]

Only 11 per cent of cases were kept open for longer than six months. The Warnock Report[16] and Wilson and Evans[17] make similar comment on the limitations of social work intervention.

If these views are a true reflection of national provision, it is not surprising that some clients, particularly the parents of children in care, do not value the intervention of social services departments as might be hoped. They will not take kindly to counselling from professional care workers if, as has been suggested above, shortage of time and consequent infrequency of contact or rapid staff turnover prevents the formation of a helpful relationship. Under these circumstances it is to be expected that care orders for the young offender have proved 'singularly ineffective as correctional measures regardless of placement'.[18] Neither is it surprising that tragic and fatal cases of child abuse, given so much coverage in the media, happen despite social services department involvement.

Sometimes clients' adverse reaction will not reflect the quality of social services approaches. Some of the best initiatives may flounder because they run counter to the sensibilities of clients. Parents and children may be unable to avail themselves of help offered in their neighbourhood without feeling stigma and perhaps resentment greater than they would experience if their child attended residential special school. They may find themselves unable or unwilling to copy modes of behaviour modelled for them by community workers. One or both parents may be suspicious and dislike home-based intervention by social workers, viewing this as an unjust condemnation of their own child-rearing methods, perhaps undermining their self-concept. Further, many will be reluctant or perhaps, through other commitments, unable to attend day centres or family rehabilitation units or to admit family aides into their houses. Similarly the parents of the physically handicapped, through transport problems or other calls on their time, might experience difficulties in taking their child to local medical centres for therapy.

On occasion, both child and parent might see the positive advantages of boarding education appreciated by the many thousands of parents paying for their children to attend public schools. They may also accept the view that educational success is an effective antidote to emotional and behavioural difficulties, and that this is most likely to be provided in a residential environment.

SHORTCOMINGS OF INTERMEDIATE TREATMENT

Dissatisfaction with the expense of CHEs and concern at high rates of recidivism among leavers, prompted the rapid expansion of IT programmes. The full potential of these or similar schemes which could be run by education departments has yet to be realised. In the first fifteen years of its existence IT has tended to concentrate on the youngster *after* he has offended. Furthermore, early accounts of its development note other shortcomings. A wide-ranging 1978 survey revealed a lack of specificity about aims, objectives, methods and necessary training requirements for staff, as well as antipathy between social workers, probation officers and teachers.[19] The service was widely used in some areas but ignored in others. Within individual authorities there could be conflicting opinion about its value. One had a well-developed service, yet its Observation and Assessment Centres did not make one recommendation to the courts in a six-month period for a child to receive IT. In the same time-span a day assessment centre in Northern Ireland made only one recommendation out of fifty cases for a youngster to receive residential training, while community intervention was provided for the rest.

The DHSS Development Group warned in the early days of IT that it was 'not likely to be adequate for the child whose difficulties of personality are severe or deep rooted, whose home and family problems are intractable, or who has specific mental and physical handicap'.[20] Hopefully this description is too pessimistic, as it encompasses the majority of children attending residential special education. Yet it does point to IT's limited usefulness. Usually programmes only occupy a youngster for a few hours a week, do not give the family and child long periods apart which can be useful for 'cooling off' and reawakening dormant affection. Neither does it split the child from the negative influences of the peer group which perhaps led him into trouble. The problems he may be presenting at day school might remain untouched. It is unlikely to stop persistent truancy from day school as boarding education does, and might not be sufficiently attractive to ensure regular attendance at evening and weekend sessions.

Hampered by poor staffing ratios and facilities, social workers can find it difficult to create the conditions in which helpful group work can take place. One account of a Scottish IT group describes the slow painful process by which leaders had to lessen their desire for a democratic group, motivated by the sensible initiatives of the children themselves. Early idealism floundered in a 'tyranny of structurelessness'.[21] Similarly, Holman's assistant complained that too often he had to adopt the role of the policeman.[22] Helpful relationships and mutual respect between child and adult take time to develop. IT workers cannot achieve in a few weeks what residential workers will sometimes set themselves years to establish.

Perhaps a clearer role is emerging for IT and its ability to prevent the need for residential care is being more widely exploited. For some client children and their families it does work satisfactorily. However, for IT to have a lasting effect on families, it seems that a commitment is required of staff far beyond the usual call of duty, as was shown by the Bath project where Holman worked as much with parents as with the children, lived within a few yards of the client families and was accessible to them almost all his waking hours. His dedication evoked a good response from clients. Whether on tight budgets, low staffing levels and poor facilities, many social services departments can work to these standards seems doubtful. It should also be noted that accounts of the Bath project's success rely on opinion rather than scientific data.

So, on balance, how does IT measure up against residential special education as a method of relieving family stress and changing a child's perhaps negative attitudes to schooling? To answer this question it is necessary to look at the particular needs of a child and his family and the merits of the IT programmes and day education available to him *in his own neighbourhood* and to compare these to the quality of residential schools within reasonable reach of his home. Simply stated, for some, IT appended to day education will be sufficient, but for others it will not. Where parents have difficulty in controlling the child, severe friction in the home could continue and a youngster's delinquent behaviour around his neighbourhood may be unchecked. If the child does not go to boarding school he might have to be taken into long-term care by the local authority, with all its attendant stigma. Residential schooling punctuated by regular holidays and weekends at home which keep the parent and child 'in tune' with each other's lives and meet their emotional needs can often be the more attractive option.

SHORTCOMINGS OF FOSTERING

For those who do enter care, the idea of fostering might be mooted in preference to residential education or placement in a children's home. In many cases this should be encouraged, but it should not be forgotten that fostering can be problematic for social services department, children, foster parents and natural parents.

Limited availability is witnessed by expensive advertisements in national newspapers placed there in sometimes desperate attempts to find homes. While it has proved possible to foster some of the most severely handicapped children,[23] it remains difficult particularly for teenagers with learning difficulties or a history of disturbed behaviour, and perhaps with unsuccessful foster placements behind them. Even when a realistic salary is offered to attract professional foster parents, demand is likely to outstrip supply of suitable adults, as the Kent scheme found.

The Kent scheme also showed that many children posed their host family severe problems. Some children continued to cause difficulties at day school, ran away from home or became involved in drinking and fighting, leading to police intervention. These experiences were echoed in Barnardo's North East Family Placement Project where there were cases of stealing cars, solvent abuse, sexual difficulties and truancy.[24]

Emotional difficulties might be made worse by the possible culture shock of their placements. The Kent project showed that, on occasion, far from enabling a child to remain in his own community, fostering in fact transported the working-class town child to a contrasting distant, middle-class, rural setting — possibly more alien in culture and further away from home than a boarding-school alternative. Consequently, the problems of rehabilitating the child on leaving care are similar to those facing children leaving boarding school.

Placements can break down because of some children's dislike for living in a different family, with its inbuilt demands for emotional closeness. They prefer the diffuse, less intense relationships which are likely to be required in a children's home or boarding school. For a few boys and girls, sometimes described as 'adult aversive', a large staff is preferable, offering a better chance of picking a grown-up to whom they feel they can form an attachment and risk friendship. It is easier to withdraw from and re-enter relationships without painful consequence. The alternative nurturing system of group living in residential care can better meet their social and emotional needs.

Some foster couples alter the emotional or physical environment which at first had proved satisfactory for the fostered child. Host families might enter the trauma of divorce, experience intense problems with their own children, have financial problems, or move house from the area in which the fostered child had settled and made friends.

Fostering can also be resisted by the child's natural parents, who might find it more painful and insulting, and feel guilty if their son or daughter is placed in the heart of another family rather than in a residential school where staff are likely to be seen as less of a threat. This will be particularly true if residential placement removes the need for the child to enter or to remain in care. It is more comforting for parents to think of their child's problems as springing primarily from educational causes, rather than inadequate parenting as placing their child in foster care suggests.

Natural parents will also object to the common view of many foster parents, who see the child in their care as their own and consequently resent the 'interference' of the child's actual mother or father. The latter might see their child's growing affection for his foster parents and heightened dissatisfaction with themselves. Further, they notice that the quality of foster provision can be variable and that the standard of the marginal home in which their child is placed can be inferior to those of a boarding-school alternative.

In short, fostering, whether 'ordinary' or professional, while working well for some children, is not a panacea.[25] It is most valuable for some youngsters 'in care' who would otherwise have to live the year round in children's homes without experiencing family life at all. As most boarding-school pupils return at weekends and in holidays to their *own* families, it is not going to be an alternative to residential education for many.

'ORPHANS OF THE LIVING'[26]

There are also children living in boarding schools for whom ordinary and professional fostering has proved impractical, who have not prospered in ordinary or day special school, whose parents are no longer in contact, and who pose severe problems for the staff of the local children's home where they spend some of their holidays.

Tommy never knew his parents. As a hydrocephalic baby he was taken into council care. Water on the brain was cured by surgery, but he remained a child with moderate learning difficulties, to some extent disguised by his ability to chatter at length about his interests. From his earliest years, his slightly odd appearance and lack of physical ability, coupled with bizarre mannerisms, and phobias for water and dogs, attracted the taunting of other children. Teasing would be met with screaming, abuse and scratching. As he grew older, his obsessive chatter about his phobias and passion for buses and railways made living with Tommy extremely difficult. Ordering him to be quiet would only have a short-term effect. If staff were driven in desperation to trying forms of punishment, these would elicit tears and verbal abuse. Praise and encouragement for less talk and questions seemed to have little effect. Various children's homes could not manage to cope with Tommy's disruptive behaviour nor, when he reached his teens, with his sexual problems and greater violence. Day school had been tried and found wanting. Advertising locally, regionally and nationally did not produce foster parents. Residential education at a junior and then a secondary school and the loyal support of three excellent social workers were the only stable elements in his life. In boarding school, his unusual artistic ability was given free rein, he made good progress in reading and number work and overcame his fear of water. He now looks back to his boarding-school life, for all its shortcomings, with much affection for the adults and the lifestyle.

Tommy is an example of a child for whom a boarding-school life was the best chance of reasonable happiness. He remembered day school as a place of unhappiness and failure. Life in children's homes had been equally difficult. By opting for small family-group homes, staffed at times only by a RSW, his social services department had reduced their capacity to cope with childen like him. They could barely cope even for short holidays when the young, harrassed housemother, unsupported by any colleagues, was quickly at her wits' ends. A difficult situation was made worse by the local children not living in the home who would be attracted by Tommy like iron filings to a magnet, ready to bait and goad him whenever he ventured outside. Other children in the home would retreat in fright or join in the persecution.

More briefly, let us consider Jason, an emotionally tortured thirteen-year-old, who idolises his mother although she has refused to have him home for many years. He has pronounced learning difficulties, shows much disturbed, aggressive and abusive behaviour, but most intractably, despite extended psychiatric involvement and placement in a special hospital unit, counselling and behaviour-modification programmes, continues to soil his clothes and bed most days and nights. Fostering was tried and broke down quickly. Placement with an aunt also failed. Most children's homes refused to accommodate him. As for Tommy, residential school is the only stable element in his life.

Increasing numbers of such schools provide an extended year to cater for children such as these, and others with less severe problems, who in practice have been rejected by family, baffled social services, medical, day-school teaching staff and all their neighbourhood peers.

HOW MUCH CHEAPER ARE THE ALTERNATIVES TO RESIDENTIAL EDUCATION?

In a better society financial considerations would not enter a discussion on how best to meet a child's emotional and educational needs but, in an era of restricted government spending, cost-benefit analysis looms large and must enter any discussion on the respective merits of boarding and non-residential care.

It is commonly assumed that non-residential care is always considerably cheaper than boarding alternatives. It is more accurate to state that the difference in cost depends upon the intensity and duration of the day school and neighbourhood social work intervention for a child compared to the charges made by a particular residential school. The fees of the latter can vary considerably for no apparent reason; some schools run by national charities and supported by national fund-raising efforts can charge LEAs more than self-supporting and DES 'listed' independent schools of proven quality. CHEs are generally much more expensive than either, although they will be providing a fifty-two week service. It can therefore be misleading to 'prove' the expensiveness of residential education by comparing non-residential alternatives only to this latter kind of provision. Comparisons should also make allowances for hidden costs, perhaps shifted from one local government department's budget to another's and falsely proclaimed as a saving.

At one end of the care–education continuum mentioned above, if a child continues to live at home, receives limited additional assistance in ordinary school, and a social worker makes occasional calls to the family home, the contrast with the cost of residential care and education will be marked. However, such limited intervention is unlikely to meet the needs of most children at present in boarding education.

In the middle of the continuum a child might attend a generously staffed and therefore expensive day special unit, receive regular social work support and attend IT programmes some evenings. Meanwhile social workers may assist the parents, perhaps with much greater intensity than if the child had been away at boarding school, when social workers employed by the latter may have taken on the task. The financial gap narrows.

At a higher level of intensity, the parents as well as the child might receive assistance other than counselling from the social services. A Home Care Assistant may work in the family home for a significant number of hours each week, and the child may receive more intensive IT involving some residential periods. Meanwhile the child receives generously staffed and expensive special education. Some of this provision will be funded by the social services department and some by the LEA, but the costs to both should be remembered in comparing the method with residential education.

If a child is fostered and the normal allowances paid to the substitute carers, and the child receives an intensive day special education or attends a properly supported integrated programme, the difference in cost lessens still further. The Kent scheme recognised that placing the child with professional foster parents could cost as much as cheaper forms of residential care.[27] Walton and Elliott calculated that, when hidden costs are included, this scheme cost almost the same as placing a child in the most expensive form of residential education, the CHE.[28]

Properly organised, day 'special' or 'integrated' education programmes linked to intensive social work intervention are not cheap options. Only where a local authority provides inadequate staffing levels and facilities in education and social work departments might significant savings be made if children traditionally considered for residential education were to be kept in day schools.

THE BOARDING SOLUTION

If social services and education departments could unite to provide effective non-residential alternatives, bringing practical help into the overtaxed family's home on a national scale, providing direct training perhaps using behaviourist methods for parents and children, or organising extended evening, weekend and holiday IT programmes geared to meet individual needs, then many fewer children from families under stress would need the help offered by residential education. Similarly, if professional fostering schemes could be substantially extended, demand might also slacken.

However, these are stiff conditions not likely to be met in the forseeable future on a national scale. Given the inertia of established procedure and the political reluctance to cease using existing expensive facilities, in which many thousands of people are employed, it seems unlikely that there will be dramatic movement in these directions, particularly if local authorities' community-based provision, because of financial stringency, continues to fall short of the thoroughness and effectiveness needed for it to prove itself clearly.

It can also be argued that in the wake of recent child-abuse cases, where children at risk have been left by social workers in the care of their parents with tragic consequences, that there might be a move away from non-residential approaches.

But leaving aside such headline catching cases, there is a dearth of 'hard' evidence that alternatives to residential care and education are in fact better at meeting children's needs. There seems much truth in Nancy Hazel's comment that 'All placement policies are shaped by beliefs rather than by knowledge'.[29]

This is perhaps reflected in 'consumer' opinion as, even where home and community-based approaches work well, some parents and their child with special needs *choose* residential schooling in preference. Parents perhaps like to view their youngster's difficulties in educational rather than social work terms. This might be a face-saving gambit, a rational explanation of their family difficulties which avoids self-accusations and recrimination. Nevertheless, thinking in educational rather than social work terms can lead to the easing of seemingly intractable problems. Education in a well-organised boarding establishment *can* be a better remedy for a child's problems, which in essence are social and emotional, than the social work approaches described in the first half of this chapter. A change of school, of staff, of peer group and social life, and an altered educational curriculum more suited to the child's individual needs can profoundly alter the child's attitude to life. If, in contrast to the child's previous day establishments, the residential school provides the youngster with experience of successful achievement in a range of educational and social activities, his self-image will be enhanced and the attractions of his previous disturbed behaviour substantially lessened. Of course this is not likely to happen at indifferent or poor boarding schools which parents must naturally seek to identify and avoid. But, as Emma's parents and many other families have found, and children without parents, such as Tommy, have soon realised, well-organised boarding education can offer renewed hope, emotional support and a happy lifestyle as well as effectively helping children's educational and social development and, at the same time, bringing urgently needed relief to overtaxed families. It is never likely to be the perfect answer, but it might often be a realistic 'second best'.

NOTES

1. Committee of Enquiry into the Education of Handicapped Children and Young People, *Special Educational Needs* (Warnock Report), Cmnd. 7212, HMSO, London, 1978, para. 9.1, p. 150.
2. Ibid., para. 9.39, p. 161.
3. M.C. Jones, *Behaviour Problems in Handicapped Children*, Souvenir Press, London, 1983, p. 205.
4. M. Philp and D. Duckworth, *Children with Disabilities and their Families — a Review of Research*, NFER-Nelson, Windsor, 1982; see also P. Russell, *The Wheelchair Child*, 2nd edn, Souvenir Press, London, 1984, p. 93.
5. N. Schaeffer, *Does She Know She's There?*, Futura, London, 1978, p. 228.
6. *Special Education in Sheffield, 1981/2*, National Council for Special Education, 1982.
7. 'Breaking In Children', BBC television programme in *Horizon* series.
8. M. Dexter and W. Herbert, *The Home Help Service*, Tavistock, London, 1983, pp. 71–7.
9. Ibid., p. 210.
10. B. Holman, *Kids at the Door*, Blackwell, Oxford, 1981.
11. Warnock Report, para. 8.35, p. 132.
12. U. Bronfenbrenner, quoted in F. Ainsworth and L.C. Fulcher (eds), *Group Care for Children*, Tavistock, London, 1981, p. 32.
13. N. Hazel, *A Bridge to Independence*, Blackwell, Oxford, 1981.
14. Holman, *Kids at the Door*, p. 1.
15. E.M. Goldberg, R. Warburton, B. McGuinness and J.H. Rowlands, 'Towards Accountability in Social Work: One Years' Intake to an Area Office', *British Journal of Social Work*, vol. 7, no. 3, 1977, p. 278.
16. Warnock Report, para. 14.23, p. 271.
17. M. Wilson and M. Evans, *Education of Disturbed Children*, Methuen, London, 1980, p. 197.
18. Hazel, *A Bridge to Independence*, p. 13.
19. W. More, 'Intermediate Treatment Reviewed' and *idem*, 'Intermediate Treatment: an Investigation' in J.McG. McMaster, *Methods in Social and Educational Caring*, Gower, Aldershot, 1982.
20. DHSS Development Group Report, *Intermediate Treatment Project*, HMSO, London, 1973, p. 15.
21. J. Waterhouse, 'Group Work in Intermediate Treatment', *British Journal of Social Work*, vol. 8, no. 2, 1978.
22. R. Jones, *From Resident to Community Worker*, Social Monograph, University of East Anglia, Norwich, 1982.
23. H. Argent, *Find Me a Family*, Souvenir Press, London, 1984.
24. N. Dixon, C. Liddle, E. Roche and D. Rennie, *Barnardo's North East Division Family Placement Project*, Paper no. 1, 1983, p. 4.
25. For further comment on the difficulties of fostering, see R.A. Parker (ed.), *Caring for Separated Children*, Macmillan, London, 1980; J.H. Reid, *Child Welfare Perspectives*, Child Welfare League of America, New York, 1979, p. 101; J. Heywood, *Children in Care*, 3rd edn, Routledge and Kegan Paul, London, 1978, pp. 196–8.
26. Phrase used by J.H. Reid in R.J.N. Tod, *Disturbed Children*, Longman, London, 1968.
27. Hazel, *A Bridge to Independence*, p. 2.

28. R.G. Walton and D. Elliott, *Residential Care — a Reader in Current Theory and Practice*, Pergamon, Oxford, 1980, p. 3.
29. Hazel, *A Bridge to Independence*, p. 12.

3

Contrasting Styles of Residential Schools

Boarding schools come in various shapes and sizes — town house, country house, old vicarage, Victorian 'cottage' style, red brick mono-lithic, flat roofed concrete modular — and the differences in the way they are run can be equally marked. This chapter considers how dissimilarities in theory are reflected in contrasting practice. First, the psychoanalytic approach is sketched and an English example given. For a time, particularly during the 1960s, this approach was widely used in America. Discussion then moves to the therapeutic community, the post-war derivative of pioneer English 'progressive' schools which, while owing much to psychodynamic thought, differs from it in certain important aspects.

The third section consists of brief descriptions of two educational units where behaviour modification (BM) is used extensively. For the benefit of residential workers not familiar with this approach, a brief description of the major principles of BM is included. This section widens the debate from the disturbed to the multi-handicapped with severe learning difficulties, and suggests that behaviour modification can be a useful method in residential schools for children with many different kinds of disability.

A BM approach to specific problems such as toilet training would not be out of place in the much broader group of schools organised on *family-group* lines described in the fourth section. This form of organisa-tion consciously uses and adapts school buildings to meet the demands of its theoretical underpinnings. There are family-group schools for the physically and sensorily handicapped and for children with learning difficulties, as well as youngsters with emotional and behavioural disorders.

The same is true of the largest group, outlined in the fifth section under a title chosen *faute de mieux*, the orthodox approach. In this group, traditional school subjects are stressed in structured environments. Children's emotional and behavioural problems are believed to be eased by frequent experience of success and the achievement of instrumental goals valued by society beyond the confines of the school itself. Close staff–pupil relationships are important but pupils are expected to comply with traditional forms of school discipline.

The penultimate section considers arguments for and against coeducation in residential special schools — another important issue which differentiates one school from another.

In the concluding paragraphs, it is suggested that there is perhaps a developing consensus that there is good in all the approaches described. Effective schools are likely to be eclectic, taking ideas from all perspectives, paying attention to all forces acting on a child — emotional, physical and organisational, both at home and at school. This broad view has been described as the ecological approach.

THE PSYCHOANALYTIC APPROACH[1]

Psychodynamic theory is less influential than twenty years ago when nearly every American school for disturbed children offered psychotherapy. As the years have passed some sympathisers have recognised the need for revision and dilution of earlier firm beliefs based on Freudian ideas but many of its central tenets should still be heeded by residential workers.

Psychotherapists believe that one must look for the underlying causes of maladjusted behaviour which are likely to date back to the inner conflicts, unsuccessfully mediated by a person's ego, between id (a person's innate drives and instincts) and superego (akin to a person's conscience) in a child's early years, intertwined with the type of relationship he had with his parents. It is ineffective and probably harmful merely to treat the overt symptoms which may appear at school. These are likely to be manifestations of deep, underlying conflicts. If these symptoms are suppressed the person may unconsciously substitute more harmful alternatives. Children probably do not know why they are behaving badly and, even if they do, are not able to control their actions. If a teacher represses a child's overt disturbed behaviour, he may be denying the child an insight into the underlying causes. Children should be encouraged to express their feelings and teachers and care workers trained to provide environments which do not repress 'acting out' symptoms. A corollary to this is the irrelevance, if not harm, which any punishment has if applied to the usually incomprehending child.

For a full account of an English residential school for disturbed boys where these ideas have been influential and where psychoanalysis is used extensively, Otto Shaw's account of his work at Red Hill School in Kent should be studied.[2] There are strong Freudian undertones to his work. Boys' desire to smoke is seen as a kind of oral deprivation, linked to a child's faulty passage through a psychosexual stage. A child sucks his thumb as a substitute for his mother's breast. The major cause of maladjustment is seen as a child's faulty relationship with his parents. Feelings must not be suppressed: 'Acting out' is to be expected as

'it is ridiculous to expect that a maladjusted child will not show his maladjustment'.[3] This behaviour, Shaw conceded, leads to much damage to school furnishings as staff try to guide pupils towards self-discipline. Adults lead by example rather than preaching, trying to draw out of the children the ability to rebuke the sin without condemning the sinner — one of Shaw's criteria for success in older boys.

A useful way of evolving this attitude is to give the children as much self-government as possible. The pupils therefore meet together as a school or in committees to review and adjust daily organisation. They deal with their fellow pupils' misdemeanours in pupil courts. This democratic involvement is seen as a necessity.

Of great importance are the regular one-to-one sessions between child and psychotherapist, in which the inner conflicts of the child are explored, and through which the therapist hopes to help the youngster gain insight into his childhood origins. Reflecting forms of organisation in the 1960s in the United States, Shaw wrote of the school's approach to the delivery of psychotherapy: 'On the whole we have been success-ful in establishing that the treatment situation is one entirely divorced from lessons, meal times, play, work, games, hobbies, courts, commit-tees, and from all the other activities within the school.'[4] At Red Hill, unlike some early schools following a psychoanalytic approach, educa-tion is valued. Children are compelled to attend classes. Instrumental educational goals are pursued although expressive goals are seen as perhaps more important.

Shaw claimed that 67 per cent of his leavers were 'radically cured on a completely permanent and adjusted basis' and 21 per cent were much improved. He stressed that he doubted the efficacy of such methods for children with average or limited ability. All his children had IQs of over 130. Level of intelligence may be a crucial determinant of the efficacy of this approach.

Regardless of the ability level, some writers express severe doubts. Wilson and Evans claimed that after many years' experience there was still little objective evidence of the long-term benefits of psychotherapy and that it was widely felt to be ineffective.[5] Attempts to apply it to the treatment of autism, pioneered in the 1940s, have been abandoned.

However, treatment methods deriving from psychoanalytic theory helped to draw attention to the inadequacies of many child-care establishments which were over-regimented, too concerned with discipline and paid little attention to individual needs. The enduring, still sometimes neglected message remains (stripped of Freudian language):

- As personality characteristics are often determined by early childhood experiences, in particular the nature of the child's relationship with his parents, residential schools must never forget the importance of the child–family relationship.
- Teachers and RSWs should remember that the disturbed child perhaps *cannot* rather than *will not* behave. They should therefore be more inclined to forgive a child for his misdemeanours.
- The good educator will respect the importance of a child's *feelings*. He will also provide means for these to be expressed, perhaps through counselling, bearing in mind the psychoanalyst's concern for the damage caused by repression.
- *Needs theory* has evolved from writers influenced by the psychodynamic school and has sharpened residential worker's awareness of what constitutes good child care. If a child's needs for good physical care, love, security and opportunity for challenge or self-expression are not met a child will remain disturbed.

THE THERAPEUTIC COMMUNITY

While the therapeutic community has grown from psychodynamic theory, the supporters of this approach agree with Trieschmann *et al*.[6] rather than Otto Shaw. The milieu in which the child spends the other twenty-three hours is as important as the hour he spends alone with the psychotherapist. Teachers and RSWs are as influential as the psychotherapist and should, while sharing the child's 'life space', use the daily routine, from waking to going to sleep, as a medium for aiding children's social and emotional development.

An early and influential precursor of modern 'milieu' therapy is described in *Wayward Youth*, written in 1925.[7] In this, the Viennese psychoanalyst, Aichhorn, described his progressive training school at Oberhollabrunn, which he ran on very different lines to the traditional regimes for young offenders he noted around him. He criticised these for their militaristic, rigid and depersonalised routines. He complained that punishment was harsh and overused. He noted the surly, shut-in reaction of the inmates which resulted when boys were forced to damn up their emotional disturbance. He wanted a new style of school where children were allowed much greater freedom, could make a noise, be untidy, in short were allowed to behave as children in a liberal family would. Lasting change could only come from within the child; it could not be imposed by a staff on a resentful and perhaps frightened youth.

Half a century later David Wills wrote *Spare the Child*, an account of the conversion of an Approved School run on traditional lines into a therapeutic community. Like Aichhorn, he believed that orthodox programmes for young offenders were authoritarian, failed to understand the causes of a child's behaviour and did not take account of feelings or individual need. He was also critical of staff attitudes. His message was that young offenders should be seen as 'unhappy, deprived persons who need care and healing, and not as wicked childen who need to be taught to behave.'[8] To him punishment was a futile and harmful method.

His teaching is reflected in the four basic themes which should guide the running of a therapeutic community:[9]

Democratisation. The traditional authority pyramid in schools with an all powerful headteacher at the top supported by two deputies, with the children very much at the bottom, doing as they are told with little consultation or involvement, and respectfully calling adults 'Sir' and 'Miss', is viewed as inappropriate to the needs of disturbed children. They must be involved in the decision-making processes if they are to develop self-discipline and the ability to be responsible citizens on leaving school. They should be given plenty of involvement in the running of *their* community.

Permissiveness. In line with psychodynamic thought described above, a child's disturbance will not be aided by forcing a child to suppress his feelings or overt behaviour. A certain amount of 'acting out' is desirable. However, most present-day practitioners stress the need for realism — limits do have to be set by adults; on occasion strong disapproval has to be shown of undesirable behaviour. Permissiveness should not be licence for a child to do as he pleases irrespective of the consequences.

Communalism. Developing the democractic theme, if staff and children are to be partners in the community; if behavioural change in the children is to be brought about by children following staff example rather than command; and if full advantage is to be taken by staff of daily living side by side with the pupils for life-space counselling, it is believed important that all the community meet together each mealtime, hold regular meetings and share activities.

Reality confrontation. To ensure children do not believe that 'anything goes'; that they see the consequences of their sometimes anti-social actions, and that they appreciate the standards of open society, beyond the therapeutic community, it is essential that a child's unacceptable behaviour be confronted and criticised. Aspects of a child's character which might be painful to him must be examined and the child helped to understand the nature of his disturbance. This could be done by staff through individual 'life-space counselling' or through group pressure in meetings.

The application of these principles is believed by those who sympathise with David Wills to be the only effective way of bringing about *lasting* beneficial change in disturbed children in a boarding school. However, only a little evidence on the value of the therapeutic approach exists. Some of this is reported favourably by Robert Laslett.[10]

Other writers look on this approach with less sympathy. Millham *et al.* observed two therapeutic Approved Schools around 1970.[11] The permissive regimes were seen as encouraging unnecessary 'acting out', which was copied by other pupils. Unable to understand the therapeutic principles of the schools, pupils enjoyed manipulating staff and each other. The child-centred educational approach did not produce as much commitment or interest in classwork as more traditional teaching, and success in instrumental goal attainment was poor in comparison with other Approved Schools. In one school absconding was rife. Staff, few of whom were trained in psychological methods, found daily living very stressful.

The authors noted the methods of controlling children — talking to them, appealing to reason — which characterised these schools reflected the advice of much recent writing on child-care practice. Such an approach tended to be despised by the children, who much preferred what they perceived as strict but fair teachers. Millham *et al.* noted 'the curious paradox' that the boys themselves preferred punishment as a method of control, although they knew the effects of this approach had not lastingly induced good behaviour in them in the past.

My own short experience in a junior school claiming to be a therapeutic community, although not in an extreme form, indicated a happy school which children compared favourably with their previous day schools. They enjoyed close relationships with many teachers and RSWs and wanted to work hard in lessons taken by what they perceived as capable and interested teachers. They were proud of the school and a small sample scored highly on a self-esteem test.[12] However, managing lively children by these methods was an exhausting process; children would rarely comply with staff wishes on the first request. Noise levels around the buildings out of class gave staff little chance for recuperation.

SCHOOLS WHERE BEHAVIOUR MODIFICATION PLAYS A MAJOR PART

Methods derived from behaviourist theory have grown rapidly in popularity since 1960 and are now more widely used by residential workers than psychodynamic theory. Scientists prefer it because of its sounder empirical base.[13] Central to the behaviourist position are the following beliefs.

- All behaviour is determined by its consequences: if the latter are pleasurable, the frequency of a behaviour is likely to be increased; if unpleasurable, it will decrease.
- Behavioural disorders have been learned and maintained by reinforcement and perhaps punishment.
- In contrast to psychotherapists' belief, it is not helpful to search for underlying causes of a child's awkward behaviour; one should direct one's attention to assessing accurately what the child actually does and noting the exact features of the environment surrounding him when he does it. From this accurate description it should be possible to identify the features which reinforce the behaviour.
- A close knowledge of a child should enable the practitioner to identify rewards liked by the child, which can be used to reinforce desired behaviour.
- When a desired behaviour has become part of a child's regular repertoire, it can sometimes be generalised to other situations and artificial forms of reinforcement (such as sweets, presents) can be replaced by more natural ones (such as verbal praise).

Some would interpret this as mere common sense. It is what sensible parents and teachers do — rewarding and approving of desirable behaviour while disapproving of undesirable behaviour. However, there is a wide gulf between those who lean towards the behaviourist viewpoint, which would include most practitioners in boarding schools, and those who regularly use Behaviour Modification programmes.

Data are first collected by the worker in scientific fashion to establish 'baseline' behaviours. Complicated patterns are then broken down into small clearly identifiable components. Detailed plans are made to achieve the resulting graded goals, and rewards identified to act as reinforcers of desired behavioural change. Meticulous records will be kept, and schedules strictly adhered to.

It is not difficult for an untrained worker to acquire the skills to do this, but only a minority do. If a behaviour modification plan fails, it is likely to have done so because those operating it have not met these conditions.

These behaviourist ideas are put into operation in the limited behaviour modification schemes, for example to aid a child's toilet training, which are now used in some schools for children with physical or sensory disabilities with additional handicap. Similarly, many schools for children with learning difficulties find publicly displayed star charts linked to the achievement of clearly defined educational and social objectives a useful method of motivating children to achieve desirable goals. The children are in no doubt as to what the staff want of them, and the adults know what to assess. Clear, detailed records are produced which aid the planning of future individual programmes.

While many schools use BM in this limited way, few schools make it a major feature of their approach. Below are given two brief accounts of contrasting residential establishments where this does happen. Chelfham Mill School, Devon, is an independent junior school for children with emotional and behavioural disorders where Roger Burland and his colleagues have broken down the educational and social curriculum into small components. Therapists and teachers have to keep regular daily records of a child's performance in a wide range of areas, for example relationships, leisure activities, personal appearance and hygiene, compliance with school routines and traditional educational subjects such as reading. A child is awarded points for cleaning his teeth, folding his clothes at night, not being disruptive in a classroom group activity, or trying hard in basketball. Points gained are linked to clearly defined rewards at the end of a set period, for example, a bag of crisps or staying up half an hour after normal bedtime. The system is permeated with humour and children find it fun.[14]

Such an approach requires thorough preparation and constant monitoring by staff. Their weekly timetable must allow for the scientific recording of 'baseline' behaviour patterns and for the transfer of information from the children's record sheets to the ongoing graphs kept in record files. Senior staff need to be actively involved, monitoring and supporting front-line therapists, guiding programme implementation and checking that staff methods and attitudes are in line with official policy.

The active front-line involvement of senior staff (a theme to be developed in a later chapter) is stressed by Malcolm Jones in his account of his work at Beech Tree House in Cambridgeshire.[15] This is a purpose-built educational unit in the grounds of the Spastics Society's Meldreth Manor, helping multi-handicapped children such as Emma (see p. 20) who cannot be educated at the main school because of their severe social and behavioural disorders. Before the existence of Beech Tree House many of these children would have lived in hospitals for the mentally handicapped, perhaps for life.

When orthodox physical and social environments have not induced in the severely handicapped child the desire to learn basic social graces, a highly structured and imaginative approach such as exists at Beech Tree House is indicated.

First mention must be made of the physical environment, specifically designed to meet the needs of children and staff. Doors to the outside world are locked, lessening the amount of 'police' work. This enables staff and children to settle down to education rather than a worrying kind of hide and seek as tends to happen in some establishments for the severely handicapped, where a locked door is seen as a sign of an uncaring institution. 'Time out' rooms, cubicles in the corner of classrooms, are specifically placed adjacent to where the teacher is working to allow ease of supervision. There is a 'safe bedroom' where the bed is built into the floor and the window is unbreakable; there are no fragile furnishings and the room is electronically bugged. Perhaps this is a kind of cell, but it is preferable to a child wearing a straight jacket in a mental hospital, and only used for short periods until, as usually happens, the child realises that this inappropriate behaviour is unrewarding.

One-way mirrors are built in at strategic points in key rooms and staff are connected by radio loops to allow the collection of accurate data unobtrusively. They also enable support staff to help direct programmes. Classrooms like those in which Conductive Education for the cerebral palsied take place (see pp. 79–81) deliberately contain few features which might distract children from their work.

These special architectural features are set in warm, homely comfortable surroundings, which allow for personal effects such as family photographs and toys.

Imaginative methods have been devised for assembling data and for the delivery of positive reinforcers. Devices such as the Wee-D which detects moisture in a child's pants or the Pedestal Urine Detector (PUD) apply technology to data collection for toilet-training programmes. Staff carry around small tally counters to avoid the encumbrance of clipboards and pencils. Fixed interval timers are pinned to staff clothing to 'beep' at the correct moment and prompt the residential therapist to record a child's behaviour according to his schedule.

As rewards for desired behaviour, children are able to go to a choice of specially designed machines for reinforcement. First stop will be the token bank. The child can then use his tokens to operate the sweet or music dispenser or perhaps put his tokens in a specially converted television set, depending upon which experience he finds most satisfying.

These out-and-out behaviourist methods are an important though not dominant part of an approach which concerns itself with the child's complete 'ecosystem'. Active work with parents is believed to be essential. They are required to stay at the school, go away with the children and staff on the annual summer holiday and receive the school staff in their own home to be taught new methods of handling their child and to help the transfer of new skills from school to home. Reminiscent of the psychodynamic school is the notion of the 'key therapist'. It is hoped that the child will form a close relationship with this special member of staff, who is required to keep in regular contact with the parents, and to be their first point of contact.

The philosophy of both Chelfham Mill and Beech Tree House leaves much room for 'tender loving care', counselling, the spontaneous fun of childhood and other components sometimes said to be lacking in establishments run on BM lines. Both have a good record for transfering children to other establishments where behaviour modification does not play a major part. Skills acquired at school by BM methods are said to have been generalised by most children to their new living environments.

FAMILY-GROUP AND FEDERAL APPROACHES

In 1873, Thomas Barnardo converted the outhouses of his own dwelling at Barkingside, Essex, into a home for destitute girls. 'My first attempt', he recalled, 'really took shape as a small institute on what would now be called the barrack-system. Forty little girls were housed simply in a re-modelled coach-house.'[16] Numbers soon grew to sixty. Of necessity, the style of management became rigid and depersonalised. Barnardo quickly realised that the standard of child care was falling far short of his ideals. The choice of the building governed the form of the organisation and possibly shaped staff attitudes. He planned radical change:

> Instead of a big house with sixty girls clad in dull uniform, I would arrange for a number of ivy-clad cottages to arise, each presided over by a kindly Christian woman who would be called 'Mother'. The children should be of all ages, from the baby-in-arms to the girl well on in her teens training for service. They should be dressed as simply and with as much variety as possible, and there should be nothing in the way of uniform. Anything approaching institutionalism would be scrupulously excluded. In such a home, and in such an atmosphere, the affectionate ties of family life and family love would have a chance of being created and fostered in the experience of the children, while the daily performance of commonplace duties would tend to fit them for their future career. Surely the family is God's way, for 'He setteth the solitary in families'.[17]

In July 1876, thirteen 'cottages' were opened. The federal style of the Village Home existed as an example to be followed. It was not the first example of an approach which stressed the interaction between architecture and attitudes to child care but it was perhaps the most influential.

An essential feature of the family-group approach is that children live in small units, usually under the control of RSWs who live in a flat on the premises. It is therefore the home of the staff as well as the children. Children do not see staff 'coming to work' from a remote outside world, about which they know little, and then disappearing when they have worked their shift.

The living unit will often be physically separated from the classroom block, and some practitioners believe that importance should be made of ideas such as 'going home' and 'going to school' in imitation of the ordinary child leaving his family house to go to a different building for his education. As in the family house, the interior of the building will be divided into small, homely rooms. There is likely to be a comfortable living-room, carpeted and with easy chairs. There will be bedrooms for two or three children, not dormitories for a dozen or more. The children will have free access to a warm, inviting kitchen, often seen as the heart of the house. Here counselling can take place as child and housemother make a cup of coffee together. In contrast to Barnardo's barrack-style establishment, the building will not be clearly divided between staff and children's 'space'.

The blurring of physical boundaries should be reflected in the blurring of emotional and social boundaries between adult and child, as shown in the attitudes and organisational forms adopted by the residential workers. The need for staff to adopt authoritarian attitudes to the children should be lessened by the 'cottage' approach. Discipline should be facilitated by close relationships akin to those existing between parent and child in a stable family. The development of child–adult interaction will be aided by sharing the same 'life space', eating, performing chores and enjoying recreational activities together. In short, an informal, personalised style is the aim.

Pupils will have much more control over the small events which make up their daily lives outside the classroom. As most children in their own families within age-appropriate limits choose what they do, where they go, and what they wear, so should the boarder. Children should be treated as individuals by staff who make allowances for fads and feelings, viewing these as more important than organisational pressures such as a timetable pinned on the staffroom notice board. Having experienced this approach, the child is thought to be more likely to develop self-discipline, a capacity for planning and running his own life and thus resisting the institutionalising effects of residential care associated with Barnardo's 'barrack style'.

Some family-group schools may number as few as twenty pupils who will be split into three sections. However there is a trend away from such small establishments, particularly if mixed ability, wide age-range teaching is necessitated. It is difficult to provide a wide curriculum if the number on the school's roll only justifies three teachers. While such a school may meet children's expressive needs, instrumental goals may be neglected. However, social workers, teachers and parents should only pass judgement on a particular small school after viewing the qualities of the staff in relation to the specific needs of the child. The staff of a very small, homely school might contain one teacher of great ability with whom the child could form a close relationship, the value of which might far outweigh the advantages of a more diverse curriculum offered at a larger but perhaps less caring school. The child's expressive needs might be more important than other considerations.

'Federal' or 'campus' schools are made up of different family living units. These are less likely to be accused of narrow curriculum, wide age-range classes or the additional cost which small units tend to generate, while retaining the advantages of the family-group approach. The National Children's Home's schools at Hilton Grange, near Leeds, or Crowthorn, near Bolton, are good examples of this style. A large number of children are divided into small mixed family groups living in comfortable, homely detached houses, physically split from classrooms, workshops and all educational facilities.

The Royal Schools for the Deaf, in Cheadle, a regional centre for hearing-impaired children who also have social and learning difficulties, is a larger variant of this approach, where many 'cottages' are interlinking houses. With well over 100 pupils on the roll, sufficient income is generated for excellent physical plant and numerous staff covering a wide range of subjects and professions. The semi-detached building style, whereby 'cottages' are linked by connecting doors through which senior staff can pass easily, keeping in close contact with 'front line' residential workers and making their presence known to the children, can avoid one of the major problems associated with small discrete, living unit approaches.

Polsky's *Cottage Six*[18] described a well-respected American residential centre for disturbed children using a permissive, psychoanalytic approach but organised on a federal basis. Hollymeade's geographical lay-out and staffing arrangements were the same as many federal family-group schools, and note should be taken of the lessons learnt from Polsky's book.

Treatment took place in normal working hours in a central building, physically separate from the cottages where the youths spent the majority of their time. The organisation was too strictly departmentalised; unfortunately the best-qualified and most experienced professional staff only worked normal daytime hours, leaving untrained people with little experience to cope with difficult children in small houses, physically and socially remote from the other parts of the organisation. The result was that the most aggressive youths gained control in the cottage, creating a deviant sub-culture, a situation with which the staff had to connive to maintain any sort of order. Only when the outside researcher went to live in Cottage Six, and then wrote up his experiences, was the tyranny of the youthful 'Godfathers' realised. How many small child-care or educational establishments, staffed by harrassed and untrained residential workers, who, when in need of help, are unable to call upon senior, experienced staff respected by the troublesome childen, are likewise run by the most powerful adolescents?

Polsky argued that all the cottages and the main school should be fused 'architecturally and psychologically'. His message was reflected in DES and DHSS publications of the same decade. These urged that schools should be organised on family-group lines, scrupulously avoiding institutionalised approaches. However, they wished to see buildings which reflected the 'interdependence of living and learning'. Unlike the National Children's Home, they did not advocate that 'home' should be divided from 'school' for maladjusted children; bedrooms were to connect with living areas which connected with classrooms all under the same roof: 'Present experience indicates that, in a residential situation, where there is no longer a sharp distinction between school and home, children find it easier to accept an educational programme.'[19] New residential schools of this period, for example Princess Margaret School, Taunton, for the physically handicapped, or Feversham School, Newcastle, for the maladjusted, did follow this architectural pattern with small, homely living units mostly radiating under one roof from central educational facilities. Physical proximity of the family groups makes the task of all staff easier; junior front-line workers in charge of the units know that senior staff are on hand if needed, while the headteacher or Head of Care is able to 'float' from one living unit to another, keeping an unobtrusive eye on the standards of care. The children know that the head's writ runs throughout the school, and behave accordingly.

As a concluding comment to this section, it is worth noting that the family-group approach and its federal derivative have grown out of practitioners' actual experience, rather than the theories of doctors or scientists. Its features are easily understood, and appeal to residential workers helping children across the spectrum of special needs. Nearly every school for children with physical, sensory or learning disabilities falls into either this category or the orthodox category, described next.

THE ORTHODOX APPROACH

Finding a title for the majority of residential special schools which do not fall into the categories described above is not easy. One dictionary meaning attached to the word 'orthodox' is 'in harmony with what is authoritatively established, approved, conventional'. This broad definition will best serve our purpose, hopefully encompassing the many good, indifferent and the few surviving bad schools which do not seek to set trends or to carry on unusual historical traditions, and which view theory with scepticism until it is widely proved to work in practice. Staff are pragmatic and eclectic in approach, having a healthy respect for well established traditions.

The 'orthodox approach' includes modern derivatives of 'barrack-style' schools without any rigid, military connotation, and 'training schools', a distinctive form of Approved School,[20] many of whose features can be seen in boarding schools for children with different special needs. It encompasses the many schools described by Wilson and Evans[21] which believe in the value of traditional forms of education, such as teaching children to read and write, as a potent means of lessening a child's emotional disturbance and giving him feelings of self-worth. This approach was neatly described by one head as 'normality therapy'.[22] Though handicapped, disturbed or both, most children like to think they are normal, like to succeed in the educational activities their brothers and sisters at ordinary day school pursue, and like the praise they will frequently receive from their parents if they succeed in these areas.

Orthodox schools tend to look more like institutions than family group schools. Many will have been purpose-built before the Second World War. Others, created by local authorities following Ministry of Education advice in the wake of the 1944 Education Act, will be country mansions which have been adapted and expanded. There will tend to be long corridors and high ceilings, tiled or polished wooden floors, large dormitories perhaps with iron hospital-type beds on the first floor over the classrooms, and big echoing dining rooms where large tables are set out in rows.

'This is a school, not a home' is a comment sometimes made by senior teaching staff in orthodox schools. 'We don't want children becoming too attached to the place . . . . they can have comfort when they go home on holiday.' Where this attitude still prevails there is likely to be a lack of easy chairs, of curtains, of gaily patterned wallpaper, of carpeted floors, and of children's personal effects in their bed-spaces. There may be an overabundance of mottled spray-painted walls, of notice boards and of locked doors. Staff and pupil rooms will be clearly defined; the kitchen will be where the meals are cooked, not where children receive a snack and sympathy from RSWs.

While exhibiting some of these features, perhaps offputting to the new parent or non-professional, the school will often be a warm, caring place. Children can be settled and proud of their school no matter what the physical trappings, as long as the building is well maintained and staff are perceived by the pupils to be doing all they can to help their development.

Staff attitudes are likely to be in line with the findings of Wilson and Evans, (see pages 93–94 below) in their wide-ranging survey of teachers of the disturbed, many of them working in residential schools. Possibly because most boarding-school teachers have never worked in schools based on theories described earlier and do not have a deep understanding of these approaches, severe doubts are expressed on the effectiveness of group and individual psychotherapy, behaviour modification and drug therapy. Much faith is placed in the helpfulness of warm, caring adult–child relationships leading to insights into a child's character (without Freudian undertones), routine and discipline, scholastic progress particularly in 'basic skills' mixed with creative experiences in art and some individual counselling. The guiding principle is 'the enhancement of self-image through success'.[23]

In Millham, Bullock and Cherrett's *After Grace, Teeth* some of the training schools were more successful in this respect than the family-group or therapeutic schools. Furthermore, while training schools may officially set less store by meeting the expressive needs of the children, in practice they were sometimes more successful in altering attitudes and behaviour, inculcating an enthusiasm and loyalty to their school far beyond that of the family-group or therapeutic schools which, to the outsider, might seem to be the more 'caring'. Millham *et al.* stress that boys can 'differ markedly from adults in the sorts of regimes they enjoy';[24] many appreciate a highly structured, authoritarian but fair regime, where they are made to participate in a wide ranging educational and physical programme from rising to going to bed: 'Some flourish on cross-country runs, maths projects and endless showers, and institutions that provide these should not be viewed as less caring than those which discuss problems at length over cocoa and slices of dripping toast.'[25] The highly structured regime, where children absorb as new pupils the tradition that the teacher's instructions should be obeyed with little argument, where a clear system of rewards and sanctions operates, and where children have to participate fully in a highly organised programme of daytime and evening activities, occurs in schools for the physically, sensorily and mentally handicapped as well as for the delinquent or disturbed, as the last few paragraphs might suggest. It will not be believed that, because a child is handicapped or disturbed, he cannot appreciate the difference between right and wrong. 'Acting out' behaviour might often be seen as naughtiness which should not be allowed.

SINGLE SEX OR COEDUCATION?

Another obvious dimension which differentiates one boarding school from another is whether it is a single-sex or coeducational establishment. Parents and professionals might find it useful briefly to reconsider some of the points which this issue raises.

Strong views are sometimes expressed against single-sex schools, but these are based on little scientific evidence.[26] Believers in family-group approaches state that, just as there are boys and girls in ordinary families and children increasingly attend mixed day schools, so boys and girls in special boarding schools should grow up together. It is sometimes argued that the single-sex community leads to distorted social and emotional development, causing children either to idolise or to degrade the opposite sex and leaving pupils ill prepared to form healthy relationships as adults, causing unnecessary worry and in extreme cases destabilising the families of the future. Exaggerated claims can also be made about heterosexuals being attracted to homosexuality through denial of relationships with the opposite sex.

While most boarding schools for children with physical or sensory disabilities are mixed, many schools for the disturbed remain single sex, and show few signs of changing to coeducation.[27] Some of these single-sex schools have opened in the last decade; others date back to an earlier generation when single-sex education was considered desirable for all children.

Many practitioners in boarding schools would still accept this view and might find the arguments listed above unconvincing. They could point to the contact pupils have with the opposite sex at weekends and during holidays. A few may work in schools where children go out to mixed youth clubs, are allowed to have friends of the opposite sex, and even encouraged to invite them back to their living units. When this happens, chaperoning may be strict, but many parents would welcome this, particularly if, as sometimes happens, a disturbed child has a record of irresponsible, permissive behaviour.

It can be argued that while it might be desirable for well-adjusted day-school boys and girls to attend school together, it may not be wise to place disturbed, mentally immature but physically advanced children of both sexes in the close society of a residential school. Whereas the sensible behaviour of the adjusted may help the development of the disturbed, the influence of disturbed children of the opposite sex might exacerbate the problems of a pupil with emotional and behavioural difficulties. They would also argue that coeducation creates management problems, probably necessitating extra staff and therefore expense, as well as requiring greater regulation, which might lead to a regimented lifestyle preventing the development of young people's independent living skills. They will point to their many leavers with girl- or boyfriends, or married with children, who do not seem to have suffered from single-sex education.

Finally, some feminists now claim that both girls and boys can suffer in mixed schools. Timetable options are subject to sex stereotyping — Art and English are 'girl's subjects' while Science is for boys. Consequently, through peer group pressures, some children may shun areas of the curriculum in which they could do well. Further, boys tend to dominate teacher time and disrupt lessons to the detriment of girls' progress.[28]

More research is needed to decide which system works best for whom.

THE ECOLOGICAL APPROACH

Just as the debate continues on the merits or otherwise of coeducation, so does discussion on the relative values of the theories and approaches outlined earlier in this chapter. Some believers in psychodynamic theory tend to see behaviour modification as uncaring and mechanical; behaviourists say that it does not have to be so, and some counterattack by asking for empirical proof of the success of psychoanalysts. Believers in family-group style schools traditionally point to inadequacies observed in orthodox schools, in particular their institutionalised routines, spartan living conditions, lack of respect for individual rights, and remoteness from the outside world. Meanwhile family-group schools have been attacked for paying insufficient attention to the quality of the educational curriculum; stress on 'tender loving care' has obscured the curative properties for the emotionally disturbed child of classroom attainment.

However, perhaps a convergence of views in discernable, as belief grows in the ecological approach. For a child's behavioural and educational difficulties to be tackled most efficiently, attention should if possible be paid to all the constituents of his life. The American educator, Hobbs, argues that the child is at the centre of his own 'ecosystem'.[29] He interacts with the internal and external, physical and emotional forces which constitute his 'life space'. While improvement in any one part of his system can have a beneficial effect on other parts, a holistic approach is likely to be more effective. Both the psychoanalytic approach, which stresses forces acting from within the child, and the behaviourist, which is more concerned with external influences, have a contribution to make. Similarly, the good child-care practices and comfortable physical surroundings associated with the family-group perspective and the educational emphasis of the orthodox are equally valuable. Workers, no matter what the style of their school, should also recognise the importance of the child's family life and the influences of his neighbourhood, working where possible with his parents.

Perhaps reflecting a growing awareness of practice in other boarding schools, staff have increasingly borrowed ideas from other perspectives. Many, echoing psychoanalytic and therapeutic notions, have paid greater attention to individual and life-space counselling. Psychiatrists and school-based social workers have been added to staff lists. At the same time psychodynamic sympathisers have developed limited BM programmes for certain pupils. The staff of many 'barrack-style' schools have divided up large dormitories, carpeted and curtained living quarters, and redesigned areas for small family groups, paying greater attention to individual preferences and desire for privacy. Trained RSWs have taken over care duties from teachers. Children have been encouraged to mix with local society, and allowed to go home at weekends as staff have come to appreciate the importance of maintaining and developing home links. 'Half-way hostels' have been set up for leavers, run on family-group lines, in town settings as satellites of rural schools, to encourage children in overprotected orthodox establishments to break out of their cocooned and possibly institutionalised world.

This cross-fertilization of ideas between different styles of school and between different disability groups is a beneficial trend which should continue.

NOTES

1. See S. Apter, *Troubled Children, Troubled Systems*, Pergamon, New York, 1982, pp. 43–7.
2. O. Shaw, *Maladjusted Boys*, Allen & Unwin, London, 1965.
3. Ibid., p. 19.
4. Ibid., p. 63.
5. M. Wilson and M. Evans, *Education of Disturbed Pupils*, Methuen, London, 1980, p. 34.
6. A.E. Trieschman, J.K. Whittaker and L.K. Brendtro, *The Other 23 Hours*, Aldine, Chicago, 1969.
7. A. Aichhorn, *Wayward Youth*, Imago, London, 1951, Chapter 7.
8. D. Wills, *Spare the Child*, Penguin, Harmondsworth, 1971, p. 17.
9. J.K.W. Morris, 'Basic Concepts — a Critical Review' in R.D. Hinshelwood and N. Manning, *Therapeutic Communities*, Routledge and Kegan Paul, London, 1979.
10. R. Laslett, *Educating Maladjusted Children*, Granada, London, 1977, Chapter 10.
11. S. Millham, R. Bullock and P. Cherrett, *After Grace, Teeth*, Chaucer, London, 1975, pp. 91–4.

12. B.E. Cole, 'The Use of Residential Education to Improve Pupils' Self-Image', unpublished; MEd dissertation, University of Newcastle upon Tyne, 1981.
13. See Apter, *Troubled Children*, pp. 50–6; and J.McG. McMaster, *Methods in Social and Education Caring*, Gower, Aldershot, 1982.
14. R. Burland, address to NAHT conference, Sheffield, October 1984.
15. M. Jones, *Behaviour Problems in Handicapped Children*, Souvenir Press, London, 1983.
16. J. Heywood, *Children in Care*, 3rd edn, Routledge and Kegan Paul, London, 1978, p. 52.
17. Ibid., p. 53.
18. H. Polsky, *Cottage Six*, Wiley, New York, 1965.
19. Advisory Council on Child Care (DHSS), *Care and Treatment in a Planned Environment*, HMSO, London, 1970, p. 55.
20. Millham *et al.*, *After Grace, Teeth*, pp. 74–86.
21. Wilson and Evans, *Education of Disturbed Pupils*.
22. Ibid., p. 132.
23. Ibid., p. 200.
24. Millham *et al.*, *After Grace, Teeth*, p. 84.
25. Ibid., p. 85.
26. R. Deem (ed.), *Co-education Reconsidered*, Open University Press, Milton Keynes, 1984, pp. 19, 22.
27. The spread of coeducation is also hampered by the fact that there are six times as many boys with emotional and behavioural disorders in ILEA special schools as girls. For other groups the difference is less marked, although still pronounced; see Committee Reviewing Provision to Meet Special Educational Needs, *Educational Opportunities for All* (Fish Report), ILEA, London, 1985, para. 2.9.5, p. 84.
28. M. Arnot, 'How Shall We Educate Our Sons?' in Deem, *Co-education Reconsidered*.
29. Hobbs's approach is described in Apter, *Troubled Children*.

4

Bridging the Gap between Education and Care

The titles of the two following chapters might suggest that education and care are separate entities. In many boarding schools, work rotas, staff attitudes and backgrounds might support this notion. Teachers tend to work the day shift, while residential social workers look after the children for the 'unsocial hours'. Teachers have undertaken DES educational courses which stress the importance of children achieving instrumental educational goals, while trained RSWs have followed DHSS child-care courses placing greater emphasis on meeting children's emotional and physical needs.

In poorer schools, teachers and RSWs will sometimes define and then zealously guard their 'territory', perhaps looking down on the training and methods of staff of the 'rival' profession. Where this happens conflict and rigid forms of organisation can emerge which work against the children's interests. Therefore, as a prelude to describing the components of a sound educational curriculum and of good child care, readers are urged to think of the overlap between care and education and how the common ground should draw workers from different professions to collaborate on co-ordinated programmes for pupils to be pursued in both living unit and classroom. Readers working in residential special schools are asked to examine the organisation and attitudinal climate of their own school. Do education and care staff show a mutual respect, seeking to learn from each other's training, experience and methods? How can communication and co-operation be improved for the good of the pupils?

Whatever their background, people working in the best schools will be united in approach and show sympathy and support for colleagues, resisting any temptation to indulge in harmful petty rivalries. Teachers recognise that RSWs can be good educators and encourage them to take part in educational planning and implementation. RSWs see that many teachers *do* make good care workers and even without a background in child care can be sensitive to children's physical and expressive needs.

THE SHARED AIMS OF EDUCATION AND CARE

The Warnock Committee believed that education has certain long-term goals:

> They are, first, to enlarge a child's knowledge, experience and imaginative understanding, and thus his awareness of moral values and capacity for enjoyment; and secondly, to enable him to enter the world after formal education is over as an active participant in society and a responsible contributor to it, capable of achieving as much independence as possible.[1]

If these goals are broken down into their components they are as much the concern of the RSW as of the teacher. Let us take three examples from the first half of the quotation. A child's knowledge can be enlarged when he reads a book in class, but could equally take place as he talks with the RSW about hobbies or employment at bedtime. A child's experience can be enlarged by a field trip or outdoor pursuits expedition which could see a teacher and RSW working side by side in classtime activity which spills over into the care hours of the evening. The teacher might well be taking the role of assistant to the RSW if the latter is more skilled at a particular activity. A child's capacity for enjoyment can be enlarged by the teaching of leisure pursuits. In the good school this will happen both in class and in the care hours. RSWs will play a major part in this process.

Likewise the second part of the Warnock aims will also be the concern of RSWs. They, as much as teachers, should be preparing the child for an independent, active role in society. For the majority of children in residential special schools, particularly those with learning difficulties, a school's life skills or social education programme will be the major means of working towards these aims. It should be an integral part of both school day and care hours as residential life outside lesson time provides repeated opportunity for life-skills learning, for example making supper for the group, budgeting and cooking in the leavers' flat, getting out and about around the local community, doing voluntary work and developing interpersonal skills. The good RSW will make the most of these educational opportunities.

In their daily work, teachers may interpret the Warnock aims as concentrating more on the pragmatic and instrumental than the expressive, tending to forget that some children will show greater interest in classwork if their individual emotional needs are heeded. To balance this inclination, some teachers would benefit from studying needs theory — a basic component of social work training.

Teachers in residential special schools, like social workers, must aim to provide for children's interlinking and overlapping emotional needs. They should be aware of the four needs suggested by Mia Kellmer Pringle — the need for love and security, for new experiences, for praise and recognition and for responsibility.[2] They should also be familiar with Maslow's simplistic but still useful hierarchy of needs (see figure 4). This is wider in scope than Kellmer Pringle's as it stresses physical needs — an area which can be neglected in poor child-care establishments.

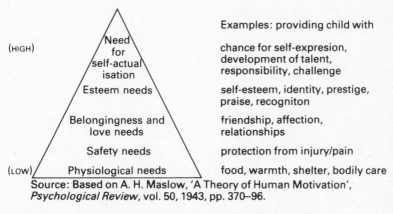

Source: Based on A. H. Maslow, 'A Theory of Human Motivation', *Psychological Review*, vol. 50, 1943, pp. 370–96.

Figure 4 The Hierarchy of Basic Needs

Maslow argues that only when a person's low-order needs have been met will he be concerned with higher levels. A child's stomach must be filled, he must be clothed, dry and comfortable before he worries about anything else. He must feel safe before he considers his desire for affection, or for a sense of belonging. If these lower order needs are fulfilled, he is then likely to be interested in status, feelings of worth, seeking challenges, or achieving goals which will give him feelings of self-fulfilment ('self-actualisation'). While the triangular diagram is an easily remembered 'shorthand' account of needs theory, and therefore useful, the sequential hierarchy is now believed to be an oversimplified theory, and does not allow for the overlapping, non-sequential nature of people's needs.

WHEN TEACHER AND RSW ARE NOT IN HARMONY

The aims of special education and child care clearly overlap, and the work of teachers and RSWs should therefore intertwine. The Warnock Committee appreciated this and noted that as a result 'The importance of close collaboration between teachers and child care workers should be self-evident'.[3] The use of 'should' suggests that sometimes this necessary co-operation is lacking — a view echoed in the Fish Report[4] and other writings.

Why should this be so? Jealousies are perhaps generated by differences in salary and holiday entitlement, which makes for latent conflict. Given present financial exigencies, there seems no easy answer to this. Among other likely reasons, two stand out. First, timetabling which arranges for teachers to work daytimes while the RSWs work evenings can mean that the care worker has little knowledge of what a child does in class or what approaches his teachers use. Similarly the classteacher who does no evening work may be equally ignorant of the work of the RSW. Communication can be extremely difficult, and co-ordination of programme planning minimal. Impressions of what members of the other profession think and do can easily be distorted by what the children themselves may allege, or by the second-hand gossip of other members of staff.

Secondly, mistrust and conflict can spring from the contrasting training or backgrounds of teaching and care staff. The importance of pastoral care and the meeting of individual needs may have been understressed in teachers' initial training, in which emphasis will have been placed on group control and the achievement of instrumental goals in the teacher's specialist subject. On the other hand, the training of the qualified RSW, probably passed on to his unqualified colleagues, is likely to have concentrated heavily on children's emotional needs and individual casework.[5] Group control, motivation and the importance of educational attainment might have been ignored. Contrasting training may give rise to suspicion and conflict in daily practice. Imbalanced attitudes may be held which make the RSW condemn the teacher's performance and vice versa.

Christopher Beedell suggested that the good residential school possessed both staff who were good at individual counselling and those who were good at group control. In his language, 'the dyadic interaction expert' should complement the 'systems expert'.[6] They should work together and not denigrate each other's approach.

At the risk of generalising from little firm evidence, it can be argued that some excellent RSWs may show a propensity for stressing individual needs while taking a blinkered view of wider group or community concerns. They may be critical of the orthodox teacher's approaches, seeing them as unnecessarily authoritarian and rigid, over-concerned with maintaining 'standards', over-critical of children, not allowing them to show their feelings. They may disapprove of teachers using sanctions and restrictions as an adjunct to group control. They may not see that standards of good discipline achieved by teachers contribute to the overall ethos of the school, and create the opportunity for RSWs to operate in a relaxed, informal manner. They may be unaware that children prefer strict teachers, as long as they are perceived to be fair and that pupils do not necessarily view authoritarian regimes as uncaring. Further they may not be aware of the important contribution the achievement of educational goals makes to meeting a child's expressive needs. The point has already been made that learning to read, to spell, to add up, to apply knowledge learnt in the classroom to everyday problems, boosts self-concept and often lessens emotional disturbance.

While the 'dyadic interactions' person might have failings, so might the 'systems expert'. Teachers, with their background and training perhaps find it easier than RSWs to organise large groups. However, in managing the group, they in turn can fall prey to bad habits which can accentuate the divide between RSW and teachers. In their desire to ensure that nothing stands in the way of helping children achieve instrumental goals, teachers can display too great a concern for efficiency and insufficient concern for individual needs. This will show up in the way such staff manage the children in class and will spill over into how they tackle everyday routines. A teacher's frequent use of sarcasm, public belittling and sanctions may make a roomful of children fall silent when he enters, and may earn him a reputation as a 'good disciplinarian'. But such methods of control are likely to be accompanied by harmful attitudes towards the children — negative labelling, low expectations and a neglect of individual differences. This teacher might view with suspicion the desire of other staff to provide for the children's love and security needs, to allow for individuality, or to boost a child's self-image. Daily routines, such as mealtimes, instead of being used as opportunities for talking, listening and building relationships, (see Chapter 6), are viewed as necesssary but troublesome events which should be organised with precision and 'got over' as quickly as possible. This member of staff will not welcome the sight of staff sitting at the same tables as the children, perhaps engaging in relaxed chatter which boosts noise levels, threatening his control of the assembled school and slowing down the consumption of food. Similarly, on an evening duty, the same teacher's style may be characterised by institutionalised supper or showertimes, with children lining up in silence, and much highly organised 'batch management'. He is likely to show a disdainful attitude to those who try to provide for unstructured play, privacy or self-expression.

If senior teaching staff are imbued with such attitudes, it is probable that junior teachers will follow their example, and colleagues who are social workers will have every reason for saying that teachers do not make good care workers and should not play a prominent part in the children's lives outside the classroom. Lacking experience of life in residential schools where such attitudes do not predominate, they may be firmly of the opinion that a clear division between 'care' and 'education' must be made.

INCREASING UNDERSTANDING BETWEEN EDUCATION AND CARE STAFF

It is important to remember that many schools do not suffer from such teacher–RSW friction. But in those which do, what can be done to improve understanding and empathy out of which can grow the close collaboration required?

If it were possible to create a completely new system, it might be advisable to follow the European model, also copied in some American programmes such as Project Re-Ed,[7] and create one profession of social educator. Residential schools would be staffed with people whose professional training covered both social work and education. The Warnock Committee was attracted by the notion of training teacher/social workers.[8] But such training would not be enough without altering organisational forms.

The common practice of timetabling teachers to work from nine to four Monday to Friday, and RSWs to cover the rest of a child's waking hours, would need to be adjusted. Examples of more flexible forms of organisation, where, for example, teachers have time off in normal school hours in exchange for evening work, do exist in this country. Other schools find that many excellent teachers do not mind working more than the normal teaching week, in exchange for a worthwhile additional duties allowance. Their evening commitment should be reasonable, at most two evenings a week. More than this might interfere with necessary recreation, make family life difficult and might leave them too tired, thus affecting the efficiency of their classroom performance. But a moderate evening involvement can help teachers understand the nature of child care, and develop empathy for their RSW colleagues. Similarly, in non-unionised schools, RSWs are happy to work extra hours for enhanced salaries and longer holidays. This enables them to make a worthwhile contribution to some daytime class activities and gives them a good insight into the methods and attitudes of the teachers alongside whom they work. If the creation of the profession of social educator is not realistic in this country, 'integrated timetabling' is, and where it exists probably helps to create closer collaboration and understanding between the two professions.

The Warnock Committee also urged that teachers in residential special schools needed training in aspects of residential child care.[9] Similarly, concern is often expressed at the high percentage of RSWs who have not followed any professional training course. Undoubtedly, suitable courses would heighten awareness. The best courses, designed specifically for workers in establishmens which provide both education and care (see Chapter 7), might improve actual skills.

However, there remains a credibility gap to be overcome in the minds of many staff. Those in senior positions who have taken child-care courses are often not able to 'sell' their usefulness to their untrained colleagues. They might recall their own experience of lecturers who have lacked understanding and sympathy for residential schools. With some justification they might fear that the enthusiasm and belief of some workers would be undermined by experiencing a course which stresses the negative aspects of residential care. They might remember the lack of perceived relevance of sections of the course which concentrated on work with old people, or forms of non-residential care or children in local authority homes. The proportion of current Central Council for Education and Training in Social Work (CCETSW) courses devoted to residential special schools is small and can give an unbalanced picture based on knowledge of social services rather than LEA establishments. Likewise, teacher training rarely include a significant child-care element.

Furthermore, for many practitioners, the prospect of leaving home and family to attend a distant college for weeks at a time as even the part-time Certificate in Social Service (CSS) course requires is distinctly unappealing. For these reasons it is important that local, perhaps work-place-based, training, for example using the expertise of the Open University, be developed probably using video technology — a more appealing method to most practitioners than lectures and note-taking. This could be linked to senior staff playing a more active role in developing awareness and understanding amongst their teaching and care staff within the bounds of their own school. Regular training days can be arranged and work rotas planned to place staff with faulty attitudes in close contact with good staff whose example they might follow. Staff meetings and the development of staff 'supervision' (see Chapter 7) can also help.

Now let us turn to another mode of tackling teacher–RSW conflict. The right kind of leadership by senior staff can make a marked difference to the degree of empathy between different professions. When Malcolm Jones opened Beech Tree House, he was determined to end the experience which had frustrated his work as a member of a large staff. He talks of the 'myth of the multi-disciplinary team'[10] where effective work is often hampered by traditional role definition. He complained of 'inter-disciplinary sparring matches'.[11] In Beech Tree he wanted a democratic, client-centred approach in which traditional job demarcation was ended. Meaningful two-hour weekly meetings were a major vehicle for achieving a 'team-wide sharing of goals'.[12] His approach is summarised in the following quotation:

> A question frequently levelled at the Head of Beech Tree House is, 'But aren't you too well qualified and highly paid to be washing up and toilet training or cooking?' The answer is a categorical 'No'. Each member of the team must know the skills and deficiencies of each child and the strengths and weaknesses of each colleague if she is to contribute fully in planning, programming and teaching. If the team leader denies herself this knowledge she becomes a mere consultant or administrator. The more remote the Head of an institution is, the less likely her goals will reflect the needs of the clients, and the staff who work directly with them. We advocate leadership by example as well as by direction, for, apart from any other considerations, inexperienced staff pick up good practices most quickly when they work side by side with skilful colleagues.[13]

Jones's approach to this work seems the most likely to achieve the close collaboration of care and teaching staff desired by the Warnock Committee. Of course Beech Tree, with under twenty children on roll, is easier to organise and lead in this manner than, for example, a regional school for the sensory impaired, with 150 pupils. In a typical school for the disturbed with forty-five pupils, the head could be required to co-ordinate a staff of thirty. He is likely to find most of his time filled with administration and relations with LEAs and parents. However, even symbolic but genuine forays into the care and education front line can have a good effect on staff morale, and can help to keep the gap between official policy and what actually happens in a school as narrow as possible. Front-line involvement gives the head the chance to observe less experienced members of staff in action with children and to demonstrate how tasks can be performed. If the person at the top cannot involve himself actively with the children or front-line staff, then his lieutenants in the upper reaches of the hierarchy — the deputies, heads of houses, and other scaled post-holders, must.

To conclude this chapter, perhaps the biggest stumbling block in the way of fusing education and care psychologically and organisationally is the unsatisfactory headteacher. The latter may be a new appointment who, by the Peter Principle, has been promoted to the level of his incompetence, or, perhaps more commonly, the long-established person, whose enthusiasm has waned or whose health may have suffered from the strains of the job. Motivation and empathy among junior staff will only be generated if the head is able to set a proficient, hard-working, unselfish example. Poor leadership and the resulting poor organisation are likely to exacerbate any latent conflict and rivalries between education and care staff.

NOTES

1. Committe of Enquiry into the Education of Handicapped Children and Young People, *Special Educational Needs* (Warnock Report), Cmnd. 7212, HMSO, London, 1978, para. 1.4, p. 5.
2. M. Kellmer Pringle, *The Needs of Children*, 2nd edn, Hutchinson, London, pp. 33–58, 81–102.
3. Warnock Report, para. 14.34, p. 274.
4. Committee Reviewing Provision to Meet Special Educational Needs, *Educational Opportunities for All* (Fish Report), ILEA, London, 1985, para 2.9.69, p. 97.
5. S. Millham, R. Bullock and K. Hosie, *Learning to Care*, Gower, Aldershot, 1980.
6. C. Beedell, *Residential Life with Children*, Routledge and Kegan Paul, London, 1970, p. 158.
7. Reported in S. Apter, *Troubled Childen, Troubled Systems*, Pergamon, New York, 1975, p. 75.
8. Warnock Report, para. 16.19, p. 300.
9. Ibid., para. 14.36, p. 275.
10. M. Jones, *Behaviour Problems in Handicapped Children*, Souvenir Press, London, 1983, p. 102.
11. Ibid., p. 103.
12. Ibid., p. 105.
13. Ibid., p. 106.

5

Education

It is possible to give in the space available only a sketch of good education practice in residential schools. It is hoped that this chapter will be of use to professionals and parents as a guide to indicators of good practice and, while covering familiar ground for some practitioners, might prompt in them some useful re-examination of approaches used in their schools.

Readers are referred to books listed at the back of this volume for fuller discussion of curriculum content and teaching approaches for particular handicaps. A study of these reveals extensive overlap. As the majority of children in special boarding have learning difficulties, important areas such as language development or life-skills training should play a prominent part in most boarding establishments for children with special needs.

This chapter continues a theme discussed in earlier pages. Educational goals are often indistinguishable from care goals. Therefore the energies of non-teaching staff should be consciously directed to enhance pupils' education. Too often the care hours are not used educationally, a point also made by Lambert in his study of public schools. Most schools he examined had academic systems which could have operated as easily in day establishments. He noted that 'the influence of residential life on the curriculum was negligible'.[1] Similarly, there are special boarding schools which confine education to classtime, believing the care hours should be devoted to relaxation, play, food and affection. But, given the educational difficulties of most children in special boarding schools, this seems an inefficient use of time. Experiences in some curriculum areas

— art, craft, sport, home economics, social education — can be presented as enjoyable leisure activities. If evening periods are allocated to these in schools where teachers play a part in the care hours and where there are few day pupils, some of the time pressures on the normal, daytime special school curriculum can be relieved.

A SUITABLE LEARNING ENVIRONMENT

While human qualities are more important determinants of the standard of boarding education, the influence of the physical setting should be recognised. Good teaching can take place in old, cramped classrooms and bad teaching in the newest facility. Children may feel more emotional attachment to a decaying Victorian pile at great distance from their home town than to the new community-based, purpose-built family-group school. But quality is much easier to achieve in a well-designed, spacious and adequately equipped environment.

The Education (School Premises) Regulations, 1981[2] are the most recent of a series of government regulations which, *inter alia*, specify legal requirements for playing fields, playgrounds, sanitary arrangements and, perhaps more importantly, 'teaching accommodation'. New special schools now have to provide 5.2 sq.m. for each pupil (in schools with up to 180 pupils on roll) and existing schools have to reach this standard by 1 September 1991. In addition there should be adequate space for storage. This formula does not mean that every classroom must be of a certain size, but rather that the total amount of teaching space in the school should meet this requirement. In practice, the government sometimes turns a blind eye to local authorities' shortcomings with regard to these rules, and, given financial difficulties which prevent the replacement or upgrading of old building stock, might not apply this deadline rigorously.

In the wake of the 1981 Education Act, these standards have been used as one of many qualifications for independent schools to be included on the DES list of approved schools allowed to be used by LEAs without special permit.

Obviously, providing large enough classrooms, sufficient playing fields and hard surfaced areas is only a beginning. Such regulations do not cover many important matters with which a school's governing body and staff should concern themselves. Observers visiting different residential special schools will sometimes see stark contrasts in both the basic bricks and mortar and how staff look after their school. Do they try to make it an attractive place for children to live and learn? Are classrooms bright and well maintained, with attractive wall displays? Do rooms allow for group work and for individual study? When damage occurs, as it often will in schools for disturbed children, is it repaired quickly?

Is attention being paid to children's special needs? For example, have the classrooms for the hearing impaired been designed with adequate reference to acoustics or soundproofing against intruding noise from outside the room? How have lighting arrangements been made for the partially sighted? What facilities are provided for physiotherapy and hydrotherapy for the physically handicapped?

As the observer views the physical provision he will also be checking on the standard of resourcing. Are there plenty of good quality educational books on display? Are tape recorders, computers, maths and science equipment to be seen? If not, why not ask to look in the classroom cupboards or in the resources room in which the defensive teacher might say the unseen equipment is stored? Why not ask the headteacher how much he is allowed to spend each year on educational equipment, and whether this is topped up by the governing body, parent-teacher association or other supporting body? If the school is for the visually handicapped or hearing impaired, what special teaching aids are available for use?

If audio-visual or other educational aids are stacked away, gathering dust in a store room, ask the teacher why. Perhaps the teacher uses an unimaginative approach in class which shuns concrete aids, or is not confident in the use of modern technical equipment, though knowing that this can aid pupil motivation.

Another request often put by HMI and psychologists, but rarely by parents and other visitors, is to see the school's staff list. The head should be asked about the training and experience of teachers and classroom assistants. Have appointments been made which make possible a broad, balanced curriculum suited to the needs of the pupils? An example of an unbalanced staff list was a CHE employing five PE specialists.[3] When a vacancy occurs in a school in or near a National Park, there is usually a flood of applications from outdoor pursuits experts.

Do numbers of staff meet legal requirements? The formal safeguard of staffing standards in special schools remains Regulation 15(1) of the Handicapped Pupils and Special Schools Regulations, 1959. This requires that 'there shall be in every school a head teacher, who shall take part in the teaching, and a staff of assistant teachers able to provide full-time education suitable to the ages, abilities and aptitudes of the pupils'. These vague requirements are amplified in a DES and Welsh Office document, *Staffing of Special Schools and Classes*, published in 1973 and referred to as 'Circular 4/73'.[4] This document is *advisory*, although it is often presented as though it had statutory force, and is very influential in the minds of Her Majesty's Inspectors when assessing staffing levels in independent schools seeking DES approval under the terms of the 1981 Education Act.

Instead of specifying fixed maximum class numbers for each handicap as Regulation 9 of the 1959 Regulations, revoked in 1973, had previously done, it gives more detailed advice. It recognises the increasing number of multi-handicapped children and the broad and contrasting range of problems faced by different schools which make hard and fast rules inappropriate. Sensibly, Circular 4/73 recognises that a head should have discretion in determining the numbers in each class. In the same school the most severely handicapped or 'acting out' pupils, no matter what their age, may require almost one-to-one teaching, while those with less severe problems, who have settled and adjusted to the school's regime, may advantageously be educated in much larger groups. Some heads ignore this and, in a miguided attempt to 'be fair' to assistant teachers and to the pupils, try to ensure that each class in their school contains equal numbers.

The advice contained within Circular 4/73 is viewed by the Warnock Report as specifying *minimum* requirements. Among its suggestions are the following;

- *Deaf*: six younger or eight older children in a class, if a homogeneous teaching group, 'would be appropriate'.
- *Blind*: for basic activities, a teaching group of six; in the early stages of learning braille or for teaching music (instrumental work), groups of two or three pupils may be needed.
- *Physically handicapped*: the most severely handicapped may only make progress in small groups of four or five. Groups of ten may be possible where physical or educational problems are less severe.
- *Educationally Subnormal (Moderate)*: between eleven and thirteen per group.
- *Educationally Subnormal (Severe)*: ten pupils per group is 'generally considered' suitable, providing adequate ancillary help is available.
- *Autistic*: six to eight pupils per teacher plus ancillary assistant.
- *Maladjusted*: for children with severe emotional disorders (particularly when first admitted to a school) a group of three or four is advised — occasionally one-to-one. Where children are better adjusted, a group of ten to twelve 'may be possible and advantageous'. An overall ratio of over seven pupils to one assistant teacher is unlikely to be appropriate.

It also suggested that 'adequate numbers of suitable ancillary staff' should be available. For the most severely handicapped children as many ancillary staff as teachers might be required.

Ten years later the National Association of Headteachers' Special Educational Advisory Committee requested a revised and improved formula,[5] reflecting the Department of Education and Science's new identification of children by the type of curriculum they required. They suggested that special schools catering for children needing a 'mainstream plus support' curriculum should have a teacher–pupil ratio (excluding the head) of 1:10; schools for children needing a 'modified' curriculum (which includes the large group of children with moderate learning difficulties), 1:7; and schools for children in need of a 'developmental' curriculum, 1:5. This last group includes children with severe learning difficulties. More controversially the NAHT Advisory Committee, apparently taking into consideration most boarding pupils' need for carefully structured social skills and personal autonomy training, also argues, although in little detail, that *all* children in special boarding schools should be classified as needing a developmental curriculum and boarding schools staffed according to the suggested 1:5 teacher–pupil ratio. It is suggested in addition that the numbers of RSWs should also be determined by this ratio. Not surpisingly, given the expensive implications of this claim, few schools have acted to meet the NAHT's wishes. Given present financial exigencies, the NAHT's figures seem worthy goals, but parents and other observers cannot realistically expect to see such a ratio for any but the most severely handicapped boarders.

In conclusion, at a time when teachers are being asked to be more accountable to those they serve, and when residential schools need to justify the cost of their existence and to prove their effectiveness, parents and observers have every right to ask searching questions in the areas described in the pages above without meeting a hostile response from defensive residential workers.

THE IMPORTANCE OF THE WRITTEN CURRICULUM

Good special schools are well-organised schools. An early pointer to an effective maintained school might be the quality of the information provided by it for the use of parents of prospective pupils. The Education (School Information) Regulations, 1981,[6] require that every local authority ensures that each of its schools provides full, up-to-date information describing the curricula it provides for different age groups, the subject choices available and, in secondary schools, arrangements for careers education. This should give a clear indication of aims, objectives and methods used, including detail on how the school seeks to meet the individual needs of the particular children it seeks to educate. For example, in schools for the hearing impaired, it should say whether it adopts an oral or a Total Communications approach to language development, and whether it is providing a 'mainstream' or 'developmental' curriculum.

This information should provide an easily understood synopsis of a well-thought-out, detailed, written curriculum. Absence of the latter does not preclude good teaching, and the presence of one does not ensure it; but it does make it more likely. If the written documents are of recent origin, and are the work of the staff actually involved in running the school, they are an indication of the senior staff's grasp of their task and should give a clear picture of a school's priorities. Documents should follow the usual curricular model giving

- a description of general aims;
  a listing of specific medium- and short-term objectives in the different relevant areas, not overlooking, as often happens, the need to stress the development of children's general cognitive skills (powers of logical thought, mental analysis and synthesis) and desirable attitudes, values and sensitivities;
- the programmes of learning experiences to be followed in class and in the care hours to help children attain these objectives (leaving scope for the individual staff member to make his own contribution based on his particular skills or interests); and
- a description of the methods used to evaluate pupils' progress and programme usefulness. If pupils are not benefiting as anticipated or if staff are unhappy with programmes, then the evaluation process should lead to the alteration of aims and objectives for the individual pupil or for the school as a whole.

An efficient record system is essential. Only where this exists is it possible to check that the written curriculum is actually being put into operation. The competent teacher, will not mind if occasionally a parent or other visitor 'sits in' on a few of his lessons and looks through a child's work files. If a parent is uneasy about his child's placement in residential school, this sort of direct involvement and observation will often allay his fears that the school is not living up to the claims of the senior staff.

A study of pupils' work files and reports will also reveal the extent to which classroom teachers and social workers understand and believe in the written curriculum. If a wide gap exists between the theory expounded by senior staff and the front-line practice of junior teachers, it should be checked that the head and deputies are aware of the situation. Assuming that they are, what are they doing to correct it? How do they tackle staff development? How do they assist the young teacher's learning or handle the experienced dissident's deliberate deviations?

Of course, it could be that the written curriculum is unsuitable for present needs. Perhaps the nature of the school's intake has changed. A school for the hearing impaired or physically handicapped of average ability might have become an establishment for the multi-handicapped with learning difficulties. Alternatively, a middle school might have found that it could only survive if it admitted fourteen-year-olds. Has the curriculum been updated to allow for these changes?

As the population of most residential special schools increasingly consists of children with learning difficulties so more attention should be given to determining the contents of a *core* curriculum, containing the essential skills and items of knowledge which teachers should ensure pupils fully understand and hopefully master. In addition there should be a *peripheral* curriculum containing topics and activities which it is desirable for children to be aware of, to experience and to be familiar with.[7] As a minimum requirement, the core curriculum should be broken down into small, clear objectives, giving teacher and child clarity of purpose.

Ainscow and Tweddle point out the limited capacity of pupils with learning difficulties for unplanned, incidental learning. As a consequence, 'Slow learners need a teacher who has worked out in detail and in advance what she is going to teach, how she is going to teach it, and how she is going to check that learning has occurred.'[8] The observer in the residential special school should note these authors' distrust of permissive 'discovery' methods, in vogue in the 1960s, which might still exist in some schools for children with special needs.

WHAT SHOULD ABLE CHILDREN BE TAUGHT?

The educational needs of handicapped children of average or above ability are the same as those of children in ordinary day schools. For the child under eight years of age, learning experiences should be those appropriate to his developmental stage — a mixture in a bright, stimulating environment of planned and spontaneous experiences often using sensory or physical modes of learning which aid cognitive social and physical development. Much learning will take place by doing, by playing and experimenting with concrete educational aids, carefully watched and subtly directed by the teacher. Educational experience should contribute to the development of the child's self-help skills and independence from his parents, and to the growth of social skills and the ability to interact with other childen around him. It should use his curiosity and natural desire to explore and learn about his environment. Aesthetic and creative activities will also have a part to play.

Learning experiences must be presented to the child in ways which ensure successful completion of tasks of which he can feel proud, so that his desire for further learning is reinforced. This last point is of particular importance if children are showing signs of maladjusted behaviour. After a good relationship with their parents, frequent success in socially desirable activities at an early age is likely to be the most effective antidote to deviancy.

The development of receptive and expressive language will be a major concern in a child's early schooling. Hopefully, it will be easy to superimpose reading skills on a firm base of linguistic ability. Children will also be expected to develop the usual elementary numeracy skills. If the handicapped child is bright, has not had his education interrupted by long periods of hospitalisation, and his physical condition has not made it impossible for him to work at the normal speed, these skills should be fairly well established by the time he reaches the junior age range. He should be able to follow the usual timetable subjects.

A complaint of some parents of children with disabilities in special and ordinary education is that schools do not make sufficient academic demands on pupils.[9] In part this feeling may be a reflection of their reluctance to concede that, in addition to physical or sensory handicaps, their children may be intellectually impaired or have emotional or social problems which make classroom achievement difficult. At secondary level, parents' worries in this direction may be heightened if their child is not able to take a range of subjects at CSE, GCE or new GCSE level. Small residential schools do find it difficult to provide the able child with a wide subject choice at national examination level. If the number on roll is less than fifty and covers a five-year age span, it is not possible to employ enough specialist teachers to provide this, particularly if most children are not up to examination standard. The development of residential special grammar schools, such as the Mary Hare School for the hearing impaired or Chorleywood School for the visually handicapped, is a response to this problem. These and other schools do have good records in helping the handicapped pass national examinations and meet college entry requirements.

A few schools for the maladjusted specialise in helping the highly intelligent child and are likewise successful in this direction. Others tackle the problem by arranging for the bright pupil to follow examination courses at a neighbouring comprehensive day school, a practice which might be extended. However, this can be difficult to arrange, given that the holiday patterns of different schools may not coincide, there may be transport problems, and a day school may not welcome another potentially difficult pupil. Schools should not be deterred by these obstacles if it is the only means of meeting the parents' legitimate concern that their child receives a normal education. As long as national examination passes remain the passport to employment and a yardstick of social as well as educational success, boarding schools must do all they can to help pupils attain these goals.

More typically for the child with special needs, national examinations become a realistic prospect when they are seventeen or eighteen rather than fifteen or sixteen years old. The hearing-impaired child who, despite high intelligence, has struggled to learn to read, or the physically handicapped child whose schooling has been interrupted by periods in hospital, might only then be ready to sit them. These curriculum areas are likely to loom large in post-sixteen educational courses in some residential schools or special courses in Further Education colleges.

Examination work should not be stressed to the detriment of the physical curriculum (see pp. 86–7 below) or the aesthetic. Art, craft and drama can be very popular, providing an outlet for creativity and perhaps developing hobbies which will remain with the pupil when he leaves school. The evening care hours should be used by teachers and RSWs to pursue these interests, which can be relaxing and enjoyable and a welcome alternative to long hours of watching television. If time is devoted in the evening to the creative and aesthetic, more of the standard daytime lessons can be devoted to essential examination programmes. Given the slow work-rate of many children with physical disabilities, this arrangement has much to commend it, although it can cause timetabling problems where a school has many day as well as residential pupils.

CURRICULUM FOR CHILDREN WITH LEARNING DIFFICULTIES

An examination-orientated curriculum is not appropriate for the many underachieving boarders with emotional and behavioural difficulties and the many children with physical and sensory impairments who have learning difficulties. Their education should consist of many of the components of the curriculum provided in the good day school for slow learners. The broad curriculum areas described above as suitable for the child of average ability and attainment of *primary* age will play a major part, though teaching materials must be matched to the interests of older children.

Sensory training will have a central role, perhaps to an advanced age for the profoundly mentally handicapped. Education for gross and fine motor development will also be a major concern, perhaps, following the advice of Benjamin Cratty,[10] through the medium of playground games, used to develop physical skills but also as a vehicle for assisting the development of cognitive processes and language ability. Skills of classifying, analysing, synthesising, and generalising can be furthered through a wide range of physical and mental activities, using large or small concrete aids. From experiencing different textures, remembering and sorting shapes, identifying colours, and from similar learning experiences often used as a means of teaching childen basic language, all but the most profoundly handicapped should be able to proceed onto exercises designed to promote the beginnings of reading.

Of course, language is a much wider area than just reading. It is a basic component in thinking, problem-solving, communicating with other people and generally coping with life. Language development must have pride of place in any curriculum for children with learning difficulties. Readers are referred to Brennan's account of its importance.[11] He named five crucial functions of language which residential workers should try to cultivate, whether the child is in class or in the care situation:

- language as a regulator of a pupil's own behaviour;
- language to influence the behaviour of others;
- language as an instrument of thought;
- language as an expression of feeling and emotion; and
- language as a vehicle for imagery and imagination

Brennan points out that language is most meaningful to slow learners when related to perceptual experience — to direct, sensory input from something which the pupil is *doing*. Learning is best fostered by refraining from direct instruction. It is better for the adult to ask open-ended questions which make the child think, perhaps leading to insights and conclusions which he should be encouraged to express in his own words.

Language work will play an important part in daytime classroom activity but it should also be the concern of RSWs in the evenings. Language growth can be furthered through most aspects of daily living in a residential school. Out-of-class leisure activities such as drama groups or standard routines such as preparing supper can be used as means of provoking thought in pupils — prompting them to think, to talk through problems, and to give reasons for actions.

As part of language development, reading and writing remain fundamental components of a child's education. This must be controlled and planned by the trained teacher, but parents at weekends and RSWs in class and care hours should if possible also be involved, encouraging the child by hearing him read.

The quality of teaching will vary from school to school and from class to class. The visitor to the residential school will find it hard to assess teacher skills on a short visit. However, he can check on the range of reading schemes available. He should see that their content matches the interests of the children using them. He could also ask to see records of children's performance on standardised reading tests, which most school staffs or their psychologist will administer. Are these used merely to measure attainment or, much better, to diagnose weaknesses and to help guide future teaching? What other support is available to the class

teacher? Does the school possess a remedial teacher who can take strug-
gling pupils for individual tuition? Does an auxiliary member of staff,
perhaps a child's favourite RSW, assist the class teacher, enabling the
latter to give more individual attention to each child?

Young and Tyre[12] argue convincingly that children learn to read by a
mixture of 'look and say' and phonic methods, mixed in with spelling,
listening, speaking and writing. Their chapter on 'The Process of
Reading' gives a clear account of the holistic approach and includes
useful sections on the 'dos' and 'don'ts' of teaching reading.

Helping children to become proficient in basic maths is almost as
important as developing a child's language skills and must be part of the
core curriculum. This subject is often covered unsatisfactorily. The
Schools Council Survey found that only one in eight of the *best* schools
for slow learners had a satisfactory maths curriculum.[13] Work was
usually poorly graded and insufficient attention given to practical work.
Brennan's recommendations need to be widely heeded.

While most structured work will take place under the supervision of
the teacher in classtime, all residential workers (as in the case of
language development) should make the most of opportunities which
present themselves in the course of daily living and which might help
children's number ability. Rehearsing skills of estimation, simple mental
calculation, telling the time, measuring and perhaps weighing can be
worked into many evening and weekend care situations, on the living
units or in the kitchen; projects can be carried out in the school grounds
or by going out to the local shops. Applying basic maths to everyday
living is very much part of life-skills or Home Economics teaching and
will be returned to later (see p. 80).

Both language and number objectives can be approached through the
peripheral curriculum in which aesthetic and creative subjects must
have a place. Art, singing and drama can be used to improve children's
verbal ability. Craft can be a vehicle for measuring and other
mathematical calculations. But these subjects should be more than
utilitarian adjuncts to language and maths. Whatever their level of
ability, children can satisfy their expressive needs through them. If their
reading skills or number sense is limited, they can sometimes succeed
in one or more of these areas, finding fulfilment and self-esteem.

In the care hours, there is scope for providing aesthetic and creative
learning experiences. Once again, RSWs can help children by organising
evening activity periods, sharing their own interests and talents with the
pupils. Teachers who play a part in evening life can likewise make the
most of their talents, providing relaxed and enjoyable sessions whose
educational value can equal that provided in daytime lessons.

Other areas of the curriculum which must not be neglected are the
teaching of basic science, and general and environmental studies.

Parents are usually grateful if the school will also take responsibility for sex education,[14] but their views on this must be heeded. Physical education is discussed in a later section (see pp. 86–7).

CONSIDERATIONS FOR PARTICULAR SPECIAL NEEDS

Pupils with particular disabilities will also need special attention to be given to topics described below.

The physically handicapped

How physiotherapy is provided sometimes distinguishes one boarding school from another. Usually in British schools there has been a distinct division between physiotherapy and education departments and children are timetabled to leave their lessons for short set physiotherapy and hydrotherapy sessions. There seem to be growing doubts about the desirability of such a system. Departmental rivalries and lack of communication have been alleged and unfavourable comparisons drawn between the efficacy of treatment along these lines and the methods used in other countries, notably Hungary. Some would like to see physiotherapy integrated much more with other aspects of residential school life, and perhaps made its dominant feature.

Bowley and Gardner[15] are among those who would welcome wider use of intensive physiotherapy methods such those devised by Peto and his Hungarian followers. The Spastics Society has done much to evaluate Conductive Education in this country,[16] and recommend it for some children with cerebral palsy, the most common form of physical handicap. Barnardo's are also instigating an evaluation study. Derivatives of the original Peto programme provide a complete educational course for children as young as three years old, involving intensive, highly structured physiotherapy, perceptual training, self-help and language work in a residential setting. It is not yet convincingly proven but it is hoped that development of body control (posture, balance, locomotion, manipulating, reaching, catching and throwing skills), linked to verbalisation to accompany actions performed, leads to better cognitive functioning.

In opposition to the generally accepted view that boarding should be avoided for the very young child, Conductive Education in its pure Hungarian form *necessitates* residential care and education for the very young child for one or two years' intensive treatment and for this reason is likely to remain controversial. A closely knit group of children of the same age is brought together and put under the supervision of a highly trained 'conductor' who, in Hungary, will have undergone four years' training for this role, studying physiotherapy, speech therapy and occupational therapy. She will also be a teacher and a nurse. She will be helped by an assistant. In special rooms, slatted wooden plinths are used for exercises, eating and for sleeping in a planned, neutral, distraction-free environment.

Advocates claim results far better than conventional approaches. There is no proof as yet that actions accompanied by verbalisation do help the formation of new neurophysiological pathways, but mutually supportive group work does produce effective motivation. The expert conductor becomes the focal point in the child's life, ensuring the efficient progress of the child through the carefully structured programme.

In the United Kingdom, Conductive Education is generally used in diluted form which avoids the seven-days-a-week residential placement for the three- or four-year-old child. Parents are actively involved, maybe staying in the school for some days to watch Peto methods from behind a one-way mirror in an observation booth. In this way they are helped to overcome their doubts and fears to which the spartan surroundings might give rise. The austere physical environment goes against commonly held notions of homely, comfortable living conditions assumed to be necessary for a child's happiness and healthy emotional growth. However, maybe a lesson exists here, noted in other contexts by writers on residential care[17] — children can develop more satisfactorily in environments and under regimes which adults think are harmful than in homely family-group establishments *assumed* to be more beneficial.

Some of Peto's basic principles are described in a useful booklet by Ester Cotton called '*The Basic Motor Pattern*'.[18] This should be essential reading for teachers and RSWs new to working with the cerebral palsied, whatever their school's approach to physiotherapy.

Cotton points out that physically able babies learn to use their arms and legs, to stand up, to walk, to dress and feed themselves largely by the use of a learning process which is unconscious and automatic, copying the adults around them and rehearsing skills with occasional adult guidance and intervention but with little structured teaching. The cerebral-palsied child, however, is always out of step with normal development. When he manages a new physical movement he does not rehearse it for hours on end as the unhandicapped would. Nor does he automatically incorporate it into his regular repertoire of functional body movements. Workers with such children must help the child to practice new skills in meaningful, real-life situations: 'The aim of treatment should, therefore, be to form a bridge between movement and function, to achieve a meaningful whole and so lead toward the end goal, independence.'[19]

If knowledge of how to teach the basic motor patterns is restricted to physiotherapists working in a separate department, during daytime lessons only, and possibly with poor communications with the RSWs and teachers, physical progress is likely to be limited. New motor skills might not be rehearsed, and their relevance to everyday living might remain unperceived by the disabled child. How much better if teacher and RSW are familiar with the necessary techniques and can help the children practice them in the care hours.

Cotton outlines structured schemes for developing the motor skills needed to get into and out of bed, to use a potty, to dress and undress, to wash, to sit successfully at table, to eat and drink, to turn pages over in a book, and to walk. She suggests ways of developing general grasping and releasing skills. Her approach is influenced by the behaviourist school as well as the belief that speech can reinforce and direct physical actions. The regular verbal accompaniment to intended movements of the body required by the Peto method can help to correct the faulty speech patterns possessed by many disabled children.

Whatever the approach to *physio*therapy, the quality of *speech* therapy provided in residential special schools is another factor which might help to distinguish the good from the bad. Some larger, regional schools will have their own therapist, probably employed on a full-time basis. Others, not so lucky, may have to rely on a sometimes unsatisfactory service from local Health Authority staff. This latter arrangement may also exist in many schools for children with learning difficulties who are not physically disabled, but whose speech problems may be just as severe. Whatever the school or the way the problem is tackled, the observer should ask what arrangements are made to provide individual help from qualified staff, and how the scheme devised and monitored by the therapist is communicated to teachers and RSWs. Too often there is an unsatisfactory, fragmented response to a disability which is seen by parents as a major obstacle to their child's making friends, and is a source of embarrassment and low self-esteem for the child. Speech development should also play an important part in the education of the hearing impaired, to whom we turn next.

The hearing impaired

The development of language is most difficult and most necessary for profoundly hearing-impaired children, 90 per cent of whom are reported to enter school with little or no language ability.[20] Even after twelve years' education, most have not achieved functional literacy.[21] Further, most only manage to develop speech which can be understood by their close acquaintances. These shortcomings in the education of the hearing impaired continue to give rise to impassioned debate, dating back more than a century, as to which teaching methods should be used. Parents should be aware of the contrasting approaches which result and which sharply differentiate one boarding school from another.

Historically the question was whether it is in the young deaf child's long-term interests to be encouraged to use sign language at an early age or only lip-reading (speech-reading) should be allowed. In the 1970s, many reached the conclusion that a middle position was best. They pointed out that, having been taught in schools where signing had been forbidden, the majority of school-leavers had barely reached functional literacy. They urged that 'Signed English' should be taught. This follows the grammatical forms and idioms of the English language, in a way that British Sign Language (BSL), the language of the deaf community, does not, and is therefore compatible with reading schemes designed for the hearing. However, wherever feasible, the signs used should be the same as those employed in BSL. Where possible, children should also be taught to lip-read, and speech training should continue to be stressed. This combination of oral and manual methods is known as 'Total Communication' and is supported by the British Association of Teachers of the Deaf and the Royal National Institute for the Deaf. It is felt to be particularly useful for the severely hearing impaired who have additional handicaps. Not surprisingly therefore, in a survey conducted during 1980–1 the British Deaf Association found a movement towards this approach in British schools.[22] As more partially hearing children are integrated into day schools, and the population of boarding schools consists more of the severely and additionally handicapped, this trend is likely to continue. The use of Total Communication is also strongly supported by the adult deaf members of the British Deaf Association. The BDA, however, pushes the virtues of BSL rather than Signed English, which tends to be preferred by educators.

Supporters of signing point to the numerous studies which have highlighted the poor academic achievement of childen educated in many oral schools. Oralism is said to exacerbate problems beginning at a very early age. Deaf children under five years of age do not absorb the spoken language of their parents which helps the hearing child form internal language and cognitive systems on which reading skills are built. Signing is easier to learn than lip-reading and, if taught to the child as early as possible, preferably by the parents, would help him build up these essential systems at an early age, making him more receptive to education on entering school. Meadow[23] reports that teaching signing to such young children will enhance rather than hamper the development of speech-reading, contrary to the belief of some. Less controversially, for the older child with learning difficulties, signing linked to speech-reading has proved invaluable.

Against Total Communication there is still a strong body of belief that oralism, while initially harder for a young child, ultimately helps a deaf person cope better in a hearing world. When the oralists seemed perhaps to be losing ground they received a boost from writers favouring integration. These believe that many hearing impaired will best develop language by sharing and trying to join in the *oral* environment of their hearing and non-signing peers,[24] where speech-reading is necessitated. However, some oralists would stress the advisability of the residential special school to guarantee the pure oral environment, in which children receive continuous practice from expert trained staff in lip-reading and speech-training. Perhaps if they progress well they would be able to transfer to a comprehensive at a later date, in a way a child who has relied too heavily on signing would not.

Given this unsettled debate, it is not surprising that there are some residential schools which opt for Total Communication and others which adhere to pure oral methods. There are clearly successful schools in the United States and the United Kingdom which wholeheartedly adopt an oral approach. They tend to cater for the more intelligent hearing impaired. These children will usually come from a supportive family which agrees to the child's starting as a weekday boarder at residential school from as young as four years. Many childen, including some with profound impairment, do well in such schools.

Whether a school espouses the oral approach or Total Communication, language development must be the central facet of their educational programme.

The trend away from early boarding, which can lessen opportunities for early intensive language training, is viewed by some oralists with dismay. Late entry would preclude the intensive and apparently effective nursery and infant education provided at boarding schools such as Birkdale near Liverpool. Here the timetable is arranged so that, for the first half of each morning, classroom assistants and RSWs supervise the children *en masse* for a play session, thereby developing social skills, while the teachers take children on an individual basis for short intensive language sessions. In the junior section of the school, children who have followed this early training can be observed in lively group discussions — their ability to talk and debate clearly based on well-developed internalised language and thought processes. They are not merely answering 'yes' or 'no' to closed questions put to them by their teachers.

The observer will note the use of group hearing aids. The better equipped schools will now provide the newer, liberating radio aids, which do not encumber the childen with wires and heavy earphones. Sound basic teaching methods — clear articulation, facing the class when speaking, and good use of the blackboard — are essential for efficient learning. These considerations are equally the concern of staff working in schools which believe in Total Communication. The development of lip-reading skills remains an important aim. It is hoped that children who have learnt to sign will also be learning to lip-read, gradually finding the use of signing less necessary.

It is not possible to discuss in detail the merits of different signing systems.[25] Suffice it to say that, for the mentally handicapped hearing impaired, a simple system such as Makaton (which uses BSL signs) or the Paget–Gorman system (now declining in popularity) may be all that can be realistically expected. This can be useful in the development of simple internalised reasoning and communication between child and adult. For the more able, the claims of British Sign Language (or American Sign Language (ASL), in the United States) must not be ignored. This is the chosen language of the deaf community in which the deaf school-leaver may wish to involve himself for a full and varied social life. Furthermore, about four out of every five deaf people prefer a hearing-impaired spouse who uses BSL or ASL.[26] Finger-spelling may also be taught. It should be noted that the adult deaf will switch from one signing system to another with relative ease.

Moving outside the classroom, the observer should ask how far RSWs are encouraged to use signing with children and whether they have been adequately trained for this role. Wherever possible care staff should be able to use evening time to develop children's communication skills.

Finally, have the views of parents been absorbed, and adequate work taken place with them to convince those who may have doubts of the value of signing? Have parents been encouraged to learn to sign, using the system adopted by the school, or do they use a pidgin form which might be in conflict with it?

Schools which are less clear in their beliefs are to be avoided. For example, children can be very confused where the head is a strong oralist, and makes this the official policy but his deputy and assistant teachers are secret manualists, whose previous appointments have been in schools favouring Total Communication. In their frustration at the perceived lack of progress of their pupils, they quietly encourage unofficial signing, perhaps through action songs, games or other activities where they could plead special circumstances if the head entered the room.

Whatever the school's approach, the child must experience frequent success in educational activities to encourage further learning. Advocates of signing complain that, for too many hearing impaired in oral establishments, the years of schooling are a time of frustration and difficulty, in which too much emphasis is placed on reading and writing skills highlighting their difficulties with syntax, for example, use of prepositions, tenses, idiom and sentence structure. Metcalf[27] urges teachers to use channels of communication which are less hard work for the hearing impaired — for example, visual story-telling using slides, films, videos with subtitles, or flannelboards. Reading can be fostered through the use of picture comics. The child should be encouraged to take his own photographs and use them as a basis for language work.

The visually handicapped

Doris Tooze offers good advice on approaches and content in teaching visually handicapped children.[28] Early sensory training is stressed; sound must be made meaningful and a guide to orientation; learning by touch and smell should be emphasised. Play — touching, holding and throwing toys — can help a young child identify different sounds and from where they are coming. Social and life skills are also given prominence.

As a first step in the essential area of mobility training, a child should know how to learn about his immediate indoor environment. In familiar territory, aids are not needed if the child and his family have developed habits of orderliness — so that items of furniture, household equipment and personal clothing have strictly allotted places. Life will be made easier if the visually handicapped child has developed certain 'tricks of the trade', for example leaving shoes with their laces tied together, or matching clothes together on the same hanger in a set place in the wardrobe. With practice, a child can develop a methodical approach to household tasks, for example sweeping the kitchen floor using markers or lining up with pieces of furniture to ensure that he does not go over the same area twice.

Teachers and RSWs can assist children's development in these areas, as they can in mobility training outside — first in the school grounds and then in the street and local shopping centre, possibly using public transport. Marianne White suggested that the child's parents were the best instructors of this while the child was living at home, but too often it did not take place: 'Many children are left at home, because it is easier without them. Others who are taken out are constantly held by the hand and so over-protected that the little self-confidence that many have is undermined.'[29] So the task of giving a visually handicapped child the confidence to go out and about without an adult attendant is often left to school staff. Tooze gives excellent advice on training a child to use a long cane, as well as sonic 'bleepers' and other modern aids.

The residential school timetable will make allowance for such mobility training. The extra hours of the evening can be used by RSWs to practise skills. It should also be possible for staff to take a child to his home town to help the transfer of skills to the neighbourhood he encounters during holiday periods and after he leaves. Parents should be involved in the making of 'verbal maps' by recording directions on a portable tape recorder, and also shown how to help their child to use his long cane or sonic torch.

The Autistic

Lack of space has not permitted much attention to be paid to the autistic, a numerically small group of children, often educated alongside the mentally handicapped, but sometimes, particularly if they exhibit very disturbed behaviour which causes severe stress in their families, in specialist residential schools. The discussion above on the importance of language, self-help and social skills is highly relevant to these children. However, the general reader should think a little of the particular characteristics of the child with autistic tendencies — his 'extreme aloneness' which makes him so irresponsive to the world about him, his phobias of harmless objects, his odd ritualistic mannerisms, and how these affect the kind of educational experience he should be given.

The autistic child will usually choose to learn more by 'smell and touch' rather than by 'look and listen' approaches. If he does look closely, he may be interested in only a small part of what he sees, for example an object's colour or shininess rather than its function. The interests of ordinary children or even of most other children with special needs cannot be assumed to appeal to the autistic child. He often does not benefit from the usual social experiences provided for young children which involve interaction with those about them. So the task of the teacher and RSW is largely to awaken him to life around him, to help him come to appreciate the experience found useful by ordinary children, by arousing his interest and seeking to keep him 'tuned in' to educational activities for increasing periods of time.

Verbal instructions should be clear, brief and uncluttered. Praise and encouragement must be clearly shown. An understated nod or grunt of approval will not register. Teaching is likely to be most successful if a behaviourist approach is adopted in which planned learning is subject to task analysis, 'chaining', and rewards are given frequently. Behaviour modification has been found to be of most use for the 'emerging' autistic, for example, in helping speech development. Aesthetic experiences might help awaken the autistic — light classical music and art or craft have been found to be useful.[30]

Autism remains a disability shrouded in mystery. Causation and methods of long-term remediation for the majority of children remain largely unknown, although staff in boarding schools have produced marked improvements in some children's socialisation, particularly in self-help skills. These are often best practised through the daily routines of the care situation, and are therefore a major responsibility of RSWs as well as teachers.

PHYSICAL EDUCATION

Every residential special school should provide a lively physical education programme for its pupils. Staff have a duty to ensure that every child who is not prevented by severe physical disablement develops adequate motor skills in a healthy, well-developed body. But more than this functional approach to the subject, the PE curriculum should also meet the children's major expressive needs.

PE need not involve the intellectual skills which so many children with special needs find so frustrating and associate with failure and unhappiness. The blind or deaf child can race on even terms with the child who does not have any special needs. The slow-learning youth can compete in half-marathon 'fun runs' with the best runners in his region. The wheelchair-bound child can prove himself in inter-school paraplegic games. The mentally handicapped child can take pride in rock-climbing or conquering high mountains.

Neither does physical education need to consist solely of competitive sport. For the less able child or pupil with some physical disability, to balance on a bench or learn how to throw or catch a ball can be as rewarding as winning a race, boosting self-image as the child realises that he has achieved a goal which all children strive to reach. Learning a simple physical skill is as much a part of 'normality therapy' as learning to read.

For the more able, of course, team games and competitions should be organised, as they do add interest and challenge. Sports fixtures against neighbouring schools can be fun and give pupils the chance to rehearse social skills in new circumstances — being guests in another school or meeting and entertaining visitors in their own establishment.

The extra hours of residential life provide daily opportunity for a wide range of enjoyable physical activities, pitched at levels appropriate to the abilities of particular groups of children. Teachers and RSWs should make the most of this. If the boarding school is on an urban site, perhaps ideal for life-skills and community involvement but with limited covered or outdoor space for physical education, the minibus must be used to take children to better facilities at neighbouring schools, or into the countryside for outdoor pursuits which are such good motivators of so many childen with special needs. The rural school is often well sited in this latter respect, and should make the most of its grounds and its likely close proximity to hills and rivers for camping, climbing and boating — new exciting experiences for many urban children which are usually well exploited in good boarding schools.

PREPARING FOR ADULT LIFE

The Warnock Committee stated its belief that education should enable the child with special needs 'to enter the world when formal education is over as an active participant in society and a responsible contributor to it, capable of achieving as much independence as possible'.[31] For an indication of the task facing staff in boarding schools, compare this statement with the comments of three mothers on their severely handicapped teenagers:

> 'I spoil her . . . I do everything for her . . . I'm very dependent on her and she on me . . . I did everything for her before she went away [to boarding school] . . . even fed her.'

> 'I did give him too much help for many years but then he went away to boarding school . . . he could do more afterwards and it showed me what he could do.'

> 'I help too much because it's quicker, especially if I'm in a hurry.'[32]

In Anderson, Clarke and Spain's sample, a third of the teenagers with cerebral palsy needed help with dressing while almost three quarters of them and 90 per cent of the children with spina bifida had never made a meal in the family house.[33] Similar overprotection is often given to the visually handicapped child living at home. Crosbie complains: 'The ubiquitous presence of the family car can often lead to a lack of realisation on the part of the parents that public transport is unknown territory for their offspring.'[34] Similar reports of parents not facing up to the need to develop children's self-help and life skills can be found in books on the hearing impaired. Disturbed children of average ability and childen with moderate or severe learning difficulties might not have over protective parents, but most still need prolonged instruction and practice in this important part of the core curriculum. In some schools, particularly those for the physically handicapped, well-thought-out life-skills programmes are lacking and insufficient attention given to preparing pupils for leaving school and surviving in a much less sympathetic world than their boarding schools is likely to have been.

At the most basic level, as many children as possible should be able to dress, wash and feed themselves. They should also be toilet trained, or if this is not feasible, for example if they have had a urinary diversion, they should be helped to become competent in the management of collecting bags. For the autistic and severely mentally handicapped, it is to be expected that the development of basic self-help skills will be a major concern of those teaching them for many years. But it is not uncommon for ten-year-old children with only moderate learning difficulties to be unable to dress themselves on entry to boarding school. Even teenagers of near average intelligence sometimes do not know how to fasten shoe laces or knot a tie. Similarly, some disturbed children are capable of carrying out simple self-help tasks but do not willingly do so. They will not accept the importance of personal cleanliness, failing to wash themselves thoroughly or clean their teeth as a matter of course.

Self-help ability and the correct attitudes will be most naturally and sensibly aided through the daily routines of residential life — getting dressed in the morning, sitting at table for meals, bathing before going to bed at night. Development of skills and supervision of daily practice must be the concern of the RSW. The latter should report on progress to the classteacher, who can back up his work by classtime activities on personal hygiene, self-help skills and health.

For the school-leaver to lead an independent lifestyle, or at least to make a responsible contribution to his own family's life, he should be able to budget, to shop for himself, to know a little about nutritional needs and to have the confidence to go out into his local community to buy clothes and food. In the performance of these tasks he will use language and number skills, as well as many social and interpersonal skills. Not surprisingly, therefore, Brennan sees Home Economics as part of the essential core curriculum, which can be used as a unifying theme[35] linking most non-aesthetic and non-physical areas of the curriculum. Developing a child's life skills should not be viewed as merely a part of a leaver's course confined to his last year of schooling.

RSWs and teachers should come together to plan individual programmes for children which are not restricted to classtime in a Domestic Science room, important though this might be. What better way to practice cooking than to allow a child to make his own meals in the cottage kitchen, or to wash his own clothes as they get dirty in the living-unit washing machine? Good residential schools do encourage this overlap between 'care' and 'education'; teachers and RSWs work together to plan shopping trips in town and familiarise children with supermarkets, launderettes, post offices and clothes shops.

A drawback of most residential schools is that the local town will not be the pupil's own home community or the town where he is likely to go to college, so he may be unprepared for coping with the exact situation he will encounter when he leaves school, but by planning life-skills expeditions to a range of neighbouring towns the school can help him generalise 'about town' skills to new situations. Perhaps, as he approaches leaving, staff can be detached during the holidays to visit him at home and to practice routines in his home town to ensure transfer of skills. This could be of particular benefit for the physically handicapped and visually impaired. For the latter, Elizabeth Chapman suggests that, to ease the visually handicapped teenager's start in further education, he should be taken to the college in the quiet of the holiday period and helped to familiarise himself with his new surroundings,[36] aided by embossed maps and perhaps a long cane. Staff and parents should co-ordinate their efforts to make sure the young adult can confidently find his way around new neighbourhoods and, where possible, become competent in the use of public transport.

The school-leaver will be further helped if, in his last two years of education, he goes out on a few short work-experience placements off the school premises. An establishment with good local links can provide a wide choice of such placements — in shops, bakeries, on farms, in workshops, tyre-fitting businesses, with the local council and others. It might also be useful, during his placement, for him to experience living in 'digs'. These activities should be well-planned schemes tailored to individual needs and used as a basis for classroom work for the child to analyse his experience and for his teacher to counsel him on how to improve his performance in his next placement.

External work experience can be preceded by or supplemented by internal schemes. Various jobs can be found in most schools which can inculcate good work habits and help older children develop social skills with adults other than teachers or RSWs who are well known to them. Pupils can be attached to school-maintenance and building staff, or join the cook in the kitchen or lady responsible for the laundry. A further variant is for the school to run its own industrial workshop, off the premises, which simulates real-life working conditions. Princess Margaret School, Taunton, for the physically handicapped, runs such a scheme in a unit on the local industrial estate.

Work experience should be further supplemented by a full and varied programme of visits to factories, small industrial units and offices, introducing children to different styles of work-place. The programme could also usefully include visits to sheltered workshops, day centres, protected 'village' communities and any other environment in which a pupil might one day find himself living. A large number of children will leave to go to some form of further education. Visits to such places give them some idea of what colleges exist, what they teach and what it is like to attend one. Only with some knowledge of these places behind them can they make an informed choice about what they want to do, or where they spend their time when they leave school.

In addition to work experience and visits there should be classroom programmes which explain employer–employee relations. Wage-slips could be examined and discussed, and tax and National Insurance deductions explained. This should be linked to study, at an appropriate level, of the workings of the welfare state. Leavers should know about sick pay or how to claim benefits at a DHSS office. They should also be competent at filling in basic forms, or, if lacking ability in this area, confident enough to ask for help.

The observer should be able to ascertain from a school's written curriculum documents and record cards how well a pupil is prepared for the shock of leaving and having to fend for himself. It is likely that they will not be impressed by what they find. Anderson, Clarke and Spain's study of disabled teenagers, echoing findings reported elsewhere, found that many schools made very poor provision in the areas sketched above. Parents and the pupils themselves were dissatisfied with leavers' curricula. Sandra Jowett quotes a disabled student as saying of his old special school: 'You have a sheltered environment all your life and then they kick you out and expect you to cope.'[37] This seems representative of the thoughts of many leavers from special, particularly residential, schools. The day after leaving school is likely to be a traumatic time for the many children who have become deeply attached to their boarding school, where they will have formed deep ties with staff and other children and from which insufficient might have been done to wean them. Pupils in their final year might often boast that they cannot wait to leave school, but once that time arrives, transfer to a distant and unfamiliar college world for the brighter young adult or the prospect of a rather drab existence at sheltered workshop or on the dole and living at home with their family, with whom they still might not have an easy relationship, can soon have a depressing effect which can undo much of the good work of a residential school. To ease the problems associated with leaving the sometimes sheltered world of the boarding school, staff must take pupils' preparation for leaving seriously.

Anderson *et al.* record that only five out of the eighteen schools in their sample had specific careers lessons and 42 per cent of their sample had not seen a specialist careers officer by the time they were fifteen years old.[38] Careers officers were found to visit special schools less than ordinary schools. Furthermore, the local schools psychological service was used by only 50 per cent of their sample and the Disablement Resettlement Officer by even less for careers advice. In addition little personal counselling on career prospects was offered to children with physical impairments. Neither parents nor child had a clear, realistic idea of what they might expect after schooling ended.

This situation might also obtain in schools for children with visual impairments. Elizabeth Chapman comments on the unrealistic hopes of some children and their parents, who believe they can emulate the 'wonder stories' reported in the media, of blind people succeeding in difficult professions.[39] A few may be capable of such feats and should be encouraged, but it is kinder to tell the truth to the majority who are not, at an early stage. She urges school staff to help their pupils to a realistic assessment of what they can and cannot do when they reach school-leaving age, based on a detailed knowledge of their own capabilities. If a child is going to need 'planned dependency' when he leaves, he and his family should know this fact well ahead of his last term at school.

A school-based field social worker or home–school liaison teacher, as recommended by the Warnock and Fish Reports,[40] perhaps with special responsibility for careers work and preparation for leaving, would be most useful in any residential special school. This person could be the 'named person' who would co-ordinate the various individuals and bodies who might help the school-leaver. He should have a timetable which allows the opportunity for parent counselling in the family home and perhaps for chasing up careers officers or local social workers who might be able to supervise the implementation of a definite plan for each leaver which should be drawn up with the agreement of all interested parties well in advance. Ideally it should also be part of the remit of the school social worker or teacher-counsellor to advise and support former pupils at least for the first year after their departure from boarding school.

One of their tasks might be to make leavers and their families aware of the often unconscious prejudice which employers hold towards adults with special needs. This phenomenon has been reported in the United States, and is likely to exist in Britain. Quigley and Kretschmer tell of a 1974 study which found that 43 per cent of a sample of deaf people employed in skilled or semi-skilled work were thought to be in positions not commensurate with their qualifications and training.[41] Despite reliable work performance, worthy deaf candidates for promotion were being ignored.

At least these figures stress that many people with disabilities can achieve employment and have proved to be good workers. Despite today's high levels of unemployment, a few leavers from special schools do achieve full-time-work, as the Fish Report shows.[42] If an optimistic view is taken of the future, perhaps job opportunities will improve once more. If they do, the results of a survey quoted by Brennan should be noted by residential workers. One hundred and nineteen careers officers were asked to rank twenty-six factors believed adversely to affect the work adjustment of slow learners. The eight items listed below were thought to be the most important factors:

1. Inability to concentrate and persevere
2. Lack of initiative in carrying out instructions
3. Inability to communicate
4. Inability to understand oral instructions
5. Inability to establish relationships with fellow workers
6. Inability to carry out simple maths calculations
7. Poor reading ability
8. Lack of job satisfaction.[43]

Among other complaints about slow learners were comments on their poor time-keeping, slow work-rate, and lack of personal hygiene.

This could form the basis of many an end-of-term report on children with learning difficulties written by teachers and RSWs. It does therefore suggest the correctness of a curriculum for less able childen in boarding schools which stresses the importance of the development of cognitive processes, language and numeracy, and life and social skills training. While it will not 'cure' the problems likely to be experienced in the adult work situation, it should alleviate them.

HOW CHILDREN SHOULD BE TAUGHT

The records of disturbed children entering residential special schools abound with accounts of deviant behaviour, aggression, truancy, poor relations with teachers and peers, and alienation in the day school classroom. Yet when some of these children follow a curriculum in the special school which is split into similar subject divisions perhaps aiming for the same national examinations, their behaviour, motivation and attitudes can improve radically. The explanation for this will usually lie in the *way* these children are handled by the new adults in their lives. Staff attitudes and methods are of the utmost importance in a residential school. These can be divided into those which should be avoided and positive ones which should guide staff in their daily relationships with their pupils.

Definitely to be avoided, particularly for the disturbed, are over-suspicious and constantly critical approaches which assume the worst in a child, have low expectations of him and subject him to negative labelling in front of his peers and other staff. The child will probably have experienced too many teachers in his day school who, coping under great pressure with large, difficult classes, exhibited these failings. Perhaps lack of time resulted in poor understanding and teachers' underrating the good in a child. Often the pupil will have reacted with anti-social behaviour which earned him status in the eyes of other alienated youths. This will have become more satisfying than achievements desired by teachers.

To be recommended are the characteristics of teachers suggested by Wilson and Evans. After saying that the general climate of a school was a vital factor in how well or badly a disturbed child fared, teachers described the features which made for a helpful environment. They said that in good schools for the disturbed, there were harmonious staff relationships, high morale and child-centred approaches. Against this necessary backdrop, staff had caring attitudes, showing acceptance, concern and affection for the children. This resulted in pupils' feeling a strong sense of belonging to the school. Teachers insisted on good standards of behaviour, but showed a non-punitive attitude, depending instead upon good example, high expectations and allowing childen freedom and responsibility within a consistent framework. Pupils were encouraged to talk freely to their teachers, who had to be understanding, perceptive and non-dogmatic. Allowance was made for individual differences, and teaching programmes designed to ensure that each pupil experienced the success needed to boost his self-concept. Good communications existed among staff and between teachers and parents. Schools were well organised and teachers kept good records.[44]

The same survey asked teachers to rank twenty-two aspects of individual treatment. The six most effective techniques for helping the individual disturbed child were graded as follows;

1. Warm, caring attitudes in adult–child relationships.
2. Improvement of self-image through success.
3. Firm consistent discipline.
4. A varied and stimulating educational programme.
5. Continuity of child–adult relationships.
6. Individual counselling and discussion.[45]

These techniques overlap and are interdependent. Firm, consistent and yet non-punitive discipline will not be achieved without the child's appreciating the warm, caring relationship he has with the staff. Part of creating close adult–child relationships will be good pastoral care systems, involving RSWs, field social workers and teachers. This should allow for individual counselling in the quiet of the office of the social worker or head of unit, but it should also involve the teacher's giving up part of his coffee break to chat in his classroom over the letter a child has just received from home. It will also consist of life-space counselling around the dinner table as staff member and child share a meal together. The closeness and intensity of a small residential school helps child and teacher to understand one another in a way which often is not possible in a large day school. In the good boarding school with stable staffing, in which a child might live for a number of years, it is relatively easy to provide the required continuity of adult–child relationships.

If the child knows he is understood and respected by the adult, and feels free to talk when the need arises, his self-image will be boosted. Frequent success in class will also have a beneficial effect on how he views himself. Breaking down a habitual expectancy of failure by helping the child achieve educational goals will be the major concern of the teacher. Where possible, the pupil should be actively involved in goal-setting, and attention paid to his views.

Learning tasks should be short and structured, with much opportunity for feedback, encouragement and praise from the teacher. They should be perceived as relevant to the pupil's life, perhaps making use of his particular interests. If the child finds reading difficult, ample opportunity should be allowed for discussion and oral work, perhaps using tape recorders. If the child is a slow learner, the teacher must be patient and guard against pushing the child prematurely forward, before mastery of the previous topic has been achieved. The importance of frequent revision and 'overlearning' must be recognised.

To conclude this chapter and to gauge the educational ethos achieved by a particular establishment, consider the words of Thomas Cole, a pioneer head of residential schools for slow learners, written in 1953:

> When the children are on easy terms with you, ready to tell you their troubles and share their delights and little triumphs, to have a joke with you, and to show you their letters, and yet are ready to do as they are asked willingly and to accept your judgements, then you are doing well. This sort of relationship can only be obtained when the children know, in the first place, that you are out to help them, in the second place, that you are fond of them, and thirdly, that if it is a question of their welfare or your comfort, that they will win every time.[46]

This relaxed, but controlled situation will only be achieved by an experienced and dedicated staff — another prerequisite of the effective boarding school.

NOTES

1. R. Lambert, *The Chance of a Lifetime*, Weidenfeld and Nicolson, London, 1975, p. 110.
2. The Education (School Premises) Regulations, SI 909 (1981).
3. DES, *Community Homes with Education*, HMI Series, Matters for Discussion 10, HMSO, London, 1980.
4. DES, *Staffing of Special Schools and Classes*, Circular no. 4/73 and Welsh Office Circular no. 47/73, DES, London, 1973.
5. NAHT, 'Staffing for Children with Special Educational Needs', Special Education Mailing, issue no. 1, NAHT, 1983.
6. The Education (School Information) Regulations, SI 630 (1981).
7. Discussed in W. Brennan, *Curriculum Needs of Slow Learners*, Methuen, London, 1979, pp. 40–2.
8. M. Ainscow and D.A. Tweddle, *Preventing Classroom Failure*, Wiley, Chichester, 1979, p. 17.
9. E.M. Anderson, L. Clarke and B. Spain, *Disability in Adolescence*, Methuen, London, 1982, p. 29, 311.
10. Brennan, *Curriculum Needs*, pp. 125–45.
11. P. Young and C. Tyre, *Dyslexia or Illiteracy?*, Open University Press, Milton Keynes, 1983, Chapter 3.
12. B.J. Cratty, *Movement, Perception and Thought*, Peek, Palo Alto, CA, 1969.
13. Brennan, *Curriculum Needs*, p. 100.
14. K.J.C. Lewis, 'Sex Education: the Role of Schools and Units for the Deaf', *Journal of the British Association of Teachers of the Deaf*, vol. 6, no. 2, 1982, p. 42.
15. A.H. Bowley and L. Gardner, *The Handicapped Child*, 4th edn, Churchill Livingstone, Edinburgh, 1980, p. 60.
16. E. Cotton, *Conductive Education and Cerebral Palsy*, Spastics Society, London, 1975.
17. For example, mentally handicapped in large institutions: see D.A. Balla and M.S. Klein, 'Labels for Taxonomies for Developmentally Retarded Persons' in H.C. Haywood and J.R. Newbrough (eds), *Living Environments for*

Developmentally Retarded Persons, University Park Press, Baltimore, Md, 1981, pp. 8–9. See also p. 54 above.

18. E. Cotton, *The Basic Motor Pattern*, 2nd edn, Spastic Society, London, 1980.
19. Ibid., p. 2.
20. R. Conrad, 'Sign Language in Education: Some Consequent Problems' in B. Woll, J. Kyle and M. Deuchar (eds), *Perspectives on British Sign Language and Deafness*, Croom Helm, London, 1981.
21. S.P. Quigley and R.E. Kretschmer, *The Education of Deaf Children*, Arnold, London, 1982, p. 107.
22. Described in *British Deaf News*, May 1983.
23. K.P. Meadow, *Deafness and Child Development*, Arnold, London, 1980, pp. 146–7.
24. W. Lynas, 'The Education of Heaing Impaired Pupils in Ordinary Schools: Integration or Pseudo-Assimilation', *Journal of the British Association of Teachers of the Deaf*, vol. 8, no. 5, 1984, p. 129.
25. M. Reed, *Educating Hearing Impaired Children*, Open University Press, Milton Keynes, 1984, pp. 88–92.
26. Quigley and Kretschmer, *Education of Deaf Children*, p. 101.
27. M.J. Metcalf, 'Helping Hearing Impaired Students' in C.H. Thomas and J.L. Thomas, *Meeting the Needs of the Handicapped*, Mansell, London, 1980.
28. D. Tooze, *Independence Training for the Visually Handicapped*, Croom Helm, London, 1981.
29. M. White, 'Mobility and the Partially Sighted' in D.J. Harvey (ed.), *Children who are Partially Sighted*, Association for the Education and Welfare of the Visually Handicapped, 1980.
30. M.P. Everard (ed.), *An Approach to Teaching Autistic Children*, Pergamon, Oxford, 1976; B. Furneaux and B. Roberts, *Autistic Children*, Routledge and Kegan Paul, London, 1977.
31. Committee of Enquiry into the Education of Handicapped Children and Young People, *Special Educational Needs* (Warnock Report), Cmnd. 7212, HMSO, London, 1978, para. 1.4, p. 5.
32. Anderson *et al.*, *Disability in Adolescence*, p. 39.
33. Ibid., p. 34.
34. R.J. Crosbie, 'The Partially-Sighted Child in the Secondary School' in Harvey, *Children who are Partially Sighted*, p. 57.
35. Brennan, *Curriculum Needs*, p. 118.
36. E. Chapman, *Visually Handicapped Children and Young People*, Routledge and Kegan Paul, London, 1978, p. 139.
37. S. Jowett, *Young Disabled People*, NFER-Nelson, Windsor, 1982, p. 80.
38. Anderson *et al.*, *Disability in Adolescence*, p. 304.
39. Chapman, *Visually Handicapped Children*, p. 127.
40. Warnock Report, para. 10.16, p. 167; paras 14.22–3, pp. 270–1; Committee Reviewing Provision to Meet Special Needs, *Educational Opportunities for All* (Fish Report), ILEA, London, 1985, para. 1.5.30, p. 37; para. 2.9.82, p. 99.
41. Quigley and Kretschmer, *Education of Deaf Children*, p. 96.
42. Fish Report, p. 105.
43. Brennan, *Curriculum Needs*, p. 112.
44. M. Wilson and M. Evans, *Education of Disturbed Pupils*, Methuen, London, 1980, Chapters, 4, 5 and 8.
45. Ibid., p. 66.
46. T.L. Cole, *Odd Men Out*, unpublished manuscript, 1953.

6

Making the Most of the Care Hours

A theme of the previous chapter was that, in schools for children with learning and behavioural difficulties, the RSW should be actively involved in the educational process. A theme of the pages below is that the pupil — particularly the disturbed child with a history of unhappy relationships with his previous day-school staff — is likely to benefit if his teacher plays a part in the care situation. The opinion of Barbara Dockar-Drysdale, echoed in the work of other writers, is relevant in this respect:

> a teacher ... who never gives a child a meal, or puts him to bed, or takes him out alone, has a much narrower field of provision open to him than would be available to him if he were to be in touch with the child outside as well as inside the classroom.[1]

In schools where it is felt, sometimes with good reason, that care duties exhaust teachers and detract from their performance in the classroom and that, consequently, care work is better left to trained and experienced RSWs, the teacher should at least fully appreciate the importance of what happens in the care hours and be in close communication with non-teaching staff. He should recognise that his success with a child in the classroom might well depend on the quality of a child's life in the evenings and weekends.

This chapter divides into four sections. First, with the aid of some historical examples, we look at what good child care is not. Then we examine what it should try to be. We look at the ingredients of an appropriate physical environment, including a brief outline of some relevant government regulations. We then turn to a description of the qualities required in staff if satisfactory child care is to be provided. Finally, we sketch the sensitive handling of daily routine.

WHAT GOOD CHILD CARE IS NOT

Sixty years ago, at a time when British reform schools (the predecessors of Approved Schools and today's CHEs) were under attack for rigid authoritarianism, August Aichhorn criticised the militarism prevalent in Austrian establishments, warning that

> We must give the pupils experiences which fit them for life outside and not for the artificial life of an institution ... There is a great danger in an institution that the individuality of the child does not develop along lines best suited to his needs but that rules are laid down in accordance with administrative requirements which reduce the child to a mere inmate with a number.[2]

In a more recent book, Oscar Myers looked back to boarding-school life for the blind child in the 1930s. One member of staff looked after sixty-five boys. He remembers iron bedsteads in spartan dormitories for twenty or more pupils; rows of boys queuing at long troughs to wash in the mornings; lining up before any activity; eating in silence, six to a bench at long oilcloth-covered tables, segregated from the girls in the school. Children were over-regimented and had little contact with parents. Virtually no provision was made for privacy.[3]

Around 1970, the Dartington Social Research Unit,[4] in their survey of many Approved Schools, still found establishments which were custodial and punitive in outlook, dominated by organisational goals and characterised by lining up, marching, meals in silence, 'antiseptic tidiness', and other indications of a very strict discipline not always accompanied by a caring and concerned staff.

They also found establishments at the opposite end of the spectrum, believing in a therapeutic approach and perhaps influenced by the ideas of Aichhorn. The children did not seem to understand the aims of a permissive, psychodynamic approach, and the staff were exhausted by their frequent 'acting out' — 'Efforts each day to control the trivia of institutional life, such as noise levels ... leave staff with few emotional resources available for the deeper pastoral demands of children.'[5] The authors sadly noted that these establishments tried to follow current social services teaching on child care.

For a further example of unsatisfactory practice, think once more of 'Cottage Six'. In the daytime the disturbed children received psychotherapy and education from senior staff. Unfortunately, these experienced and trained people 'fade from the picture with the setting sun',[6] leaving the most difficult children in the hands of unqualified, inexperienced houseparents in a living unit which is architecturally separated from the main school. The boys took over; the staff could only survive by colluding with the physically strongest boys who had established themselves by aggression at the top of a vicious pecking order. A deviant sub-culture existed which was passed on from one group of boys to their successors. Delinquents became more disturbed and the 'scapegoats' and 'bushboys' at the bottom of the pecking order were persecuted. Where staff are not fully in control of disturbed pupils, this outcome is likely to be repeated. Fortunately, as the Dartington team and the Schools Council[7] survey suggest, this rarely happens.

These examples of bad practice highlight many of the common criticisms of residential care. 'Institutionalisation' is an old and influential idea. Living in an inward-looking residential institution for a long period of time can be a harmful experience if staff force conformity and a rigid routine on inmates. In such schools, children are likely to be managed solely in large groups and the ability to express their individuality severely restricted. They will lack initiative, a sense of responsibility, and, while learning how to 'play the system' of the institution, perhaps develop behaviour which is deviant in the eyes of the outside world. They will be ill prepared for leading an independent life when they leave.

In authoritarian regimes, the organisation can too easily be altered to meet staff and not pupil needs. However, in contrasting permissive therapeutic systems, designed to be child-centred, bad practice can also emerge. An excess of 'acting out' behaviour may develop, presenting bad models for other children. Staff may be openly criticised and abused by pupils, a situation, as Denis Stott has pointed out, which is incompatible with children's needing strong protecting adults in their lives, for whom they can feel respect and to whom they can look for the clear limit-setting needed for emotional security.[8]

Historically, the cause of much bad residential practice has been the underfunding of boarding schools. How can a member of staff begin to provide good child care when he is responsible for sixty children? In less extreme circumstances, a tiny team has to adopt a rigid routine, has to impose strict regulations and enforce conformity if it is to stay in charge. Poor care resulting from lack of staff was often compounded by lack of money for buildings, fittings and equipment needed to provide a welcoming, homely atmosphere.

Underfunding was also reflected in the appalling salary levels of childcare workers. In the 1890s, the matron in charge of a Northumberland girls' home had one day off per month and received less pay than the gardener.[9] While conditions of service have improved considerably,

RSWs are still badly paid. Largely for this reason, unsuitable appointments have had to have been made to fill breaches left by the rapid turnover of staff. Untrained people, not really knowing what they want to do with their lives,[10] have been placed in positions of great difficulty and responsibility looking after the most challenging of children. Had salaries and conditions been more attractive, more able and more stable staff, capable of earning the children's respect would probably have been attracted to the child-care profession. To make the situation worse, the better paid, trained staff have on occasion opted for organisational forms which have created an attractive nine-to-five lifestyle for themselves while leaving the 'unsocial hours' to the staff least fitted to cope with the situation. 'Cottage Six' was an example of this.

Miller and Gwynne,[11] in their research into residential care for the incurable sick, categorised establishments as adopting either a 'horticultural' or a 'warehousing' approach to their task. While their concept is not transferable in its entirety to residential care for children, it might be borrowed and adapted. 'Warehousing' child care might be said to take place when the staff, perhaps demoralised and feeling exploited, make little serious attempt to do more than meet children's basic physical needs. Educational and social development is ignored outside daytime lessons and staff are content for pupils to be merely 'stored'.

This could be contrasted with the 'horticultural' approach where staff do all they can to aid their charges' development, to meet higher-level needs and to increase their capacity for independent living outside the institution. Hopefully there no longer exist residential schools which merely 'warehouse' pupils in the care hours. This has too often happened in the past, and has proved a fertile bed for growing the worst deviant sub-cultures.

A precondition of a 'horticultural' approach is a suitable physical environment, and it is to this that we next turn our attention.

'A HOME THAT SMILES, PROPS WHICH INVITE, SPACE WHICH ALLOWS'[12]

The title is a much used quotation which remains an evocative shorthand description of the essential components of a suitable boarding environment. Another telling comment is one attributed to Winston Churchill. 'We shape our buildings and they shape us.' Certainly the architecture of a building but perhaps, more importantly, the decor and state of the fixtures and fittings, do affect the morale and sometimes the overt behaviour of both pupils and staff. In one sense however, Churchill's alleged comment is inaccurate. Child care usually takes place in *adapted* premises, built in the past for other purposes or designed by architects of a different era, when child-care needs were viewed in a different light. The question usually is how well the present staff or governing body have adjusted, altered and improved their buildings to meet the present needs of the children.

Have government regulations been adhered to? The Education (School Premises) Regulations, 1981,[13] contain specific physical require- ments for boarding schools to meet. These include the following rules:

Dormitories
- There must be single-sex bedrooms in schools containing pupils over eight years of age.
- For each child sleeping in a room there must be 4.2 sq.m. of floor space; to the total add 1.6 sq.m.
- Each cubicle in a divided room should have its own window and be a minimum of 5 sq.m.
- A single bedroom must have a floor area of at least 6 sq.m.
- There should be a gap of at least 900mm between each bed.

Washing and Sanitary Arrangements
- There must be a water closet for every five boarders.
- There must be a washbasin for every three boarders for the first six- ty boarders; for every four boarders for the next forty and one basin for every five thereafter.
- There must be a bath or shower for every ten boarders, a quarter of which must be baths.
- These facilities should be distributed through a school so as to be 'reasonably accessible to the sleeping accommodation'.

Health
- There must be a sick room. If a school has more than forty boarders it should also have one or more separate isolation rooms.
- These rooms must have 'associated facilities by way of baths, washbasins and water closets'.
- A sick room or isolation room must have a floor area of not less than 7.4 sq.m. for each bed and a distance of 1.8 m between any two beds.

Living Accommodation
- There must be at least 2.3 sq.m. living accommodation for each pupil, but this can include classrooms, halls and other rooms which might primarily be described as teaching accommodation.
- There must be adequate storage space for pupils' personal belongings.

The regulations also specify that proper arrangements must be made to prevent and limit fires. In the case of independent schools, the respon- sibility for checking design of buildings, fire-proofing of doors and other arrangements is delegated to the school which, before being approved under the 1981 Education Act, has to have written clearance from its local fire officer, a copy of which has been seen by the DES in London.

In the case of independent schools, one area, which is not checked by DES and is rarely considered by parents or local authority officials, is the adequacy or otherwise of a school's insurance cover, with regard to the safety of their pupils.

The paragraphs above describe *minimum quantitative* requirements which should underpin a school's child-care provision. They make little or no reference to the *quality* of delivery of the service, or specific reference to the standard of the upkeep of the school buildings. Good schools tend to be bright, cheerfully decorated places where there is clear evidence that staff make an effort to look after the fabric. If adults take a pride in their surroundings, even disturbed children with a record of damaging property will tend to copy. Where a school's staff or governing body are lacking in motivation and perhaps purpose, there will be a tendency to put up with increasing dilapidation, and perhaps a fatalistic attitude that efforts made to improve the buildings, even in a cosmetic way, by putting displays on wallboards, or pictures on bedroom walls, will be in vain, as 'the kids will just ruin them.'

The size or age of a building can make the creation of 'the home that smiles' more difficult but is not of paramount importance. Family-group design does not necessarily ensure a better living environment than a big old-fashioned institution.[14] The latter can be split up into small attractive units. Large dormitories can be divided, high ceilings lowered, washbasins installed in bedrooms, walls brightly papered, attractive curtains and bedspreads bought; individual bathrooms created, carpets put down and easy furnishings provided. Following the advice of DES and DHSS documents,[15] the guidelines should be to make the physical environment as homely as possible. In most cases the aim is not to create luxury accommodation for children which is in stark contrast to their homes (although one or two schools deliberately buy the most expensive furniture and fittings as a sign to the most disturbed that they are worthy of the best possible surroundings), rather a sensible, homely environment in which children are comfortable and can naturally rehearse necessary life skills.

Visitors to a school should check for adequate provision for group and individual needs. What efforts have been made to create quiet, private spaces to which children can retreat when they want to escape the hubbub of group living — to pursue a hobby in the evening, or simply to sit alone with their thoughts? How much privacy has been created in the child's bedroom? Has a large room been divided, to give him at least an individualised bed space with his own locker for his personal belongings, wall space for his special pictures and perhaps his own chair?

Without such provision, a person's basic need for his own 'territory' is being denied, with likely adverse effects on his behaviour and emotional development.

Adequate indoor and outdoor space for evening group activities is another essential feature. Sometimes modern schools fare worse in this respect than many older country-house establishments. When the autumn nights draw in and weather prevents sport or outdoor pursuit trips, the care hours can pass very slowly with much argument and confrontation between adults and children if the latter have been cooped up, perhaps forced to watch an excess of television, because the living unit only has a single sitting-room and teachers zealously lock their classrooms against the evening staff. How much better the large mansion with its nooks and crannies, and large rooms which can be subdivided to allow a variety of individual and small group activities and still leave barriers of space between. When the autumn rains ease, there must also be adequate playgrounds and gardens to allow children to run off their pent up energies. Playtimes can be much easier for staff to supervise and to encourage socially desirable behaviour if 'props which invite' are provided — climbing frames, adventure playgrounds, drives for cycling, walls against which to play ball games. Again the town school on a cramped site or with nearby neighbours anxious about noise levels often compares badly to the rural school in this type of provision.

There is no excuse for the continued existence of both private and state schools which do not adequately cater for the concerns sketched above. If only a tiny proportion of an average sized school's annual costs is devoted to decor and comfortable furnishings a reasonable, homely environment can be maintained.

QUALITIES REQUIRED IN A CHILD-CARE STAFF

The Warnock Report makes the specific recommendation that in the interests of sound child care, the teacher–pupil ratios recommended by the DES in Circular 4/73 (see p. 71) should be used by local authorities to determine the number of child-care workers required by a school. HMI used these standards when assessing independent schools seeking approval to accept pupils without special permit under the terms of the 1981 Education Act. Without sufficient numbers, it is unlikely that individual members of staff will have the time or energy to display the qualities required of child-care workers, whether RSWs or teachers, described in the following pages. As research evidence in this area is lacking, this section has to be a personal view.

Liz Ward stresses the importance of the residential worker's being able to exploit the routine interactions which happen in the course of daily living between adult and child to meet the latter's expressive needs and to aid his social development:

> It is *what is going on* between the people involved that determines the quality of residential care. What the worker says and *how* he says it, what he does and *how* he does it, determines the nature of the worker/resident relationship, which in turn determines the basic mode of intervention. Every incident, however seemingly unimportant, acts as a vehicle of communication: helping or hindering, caring or not caring, demonstrating authority over the resident, or setting the scene for self-responsibility and self-development.[16]

The grown-up's words and actions will communicate to the child his degree of caring and will be the product of the adult's personality and his attitude towards his job. Most children will perceive the difference between those who show deep concern, like them and are willing to make sacrifices, and the less committed whose real interest in life lies outside the work-place. Interactions between child and the less involved adult are likely to be perfunctory, doing little to meet expressive needs. Such workers will not measure up to the standard implied by Richard Balbernie in this comment: 'Residential treatment is an art, the art of making oneself available in relationship for others.'[17] To make 'oneself available in relationship' requires commitment, unselfishness, motivation and a sincere interest in the child.

In Victorian times, Sydney Turner, the Resident Chaplain of the Royal Philanthropic School and government inspector of reform schools, wrote that he did not look for outstanding talents in his staff, rather 'earnestness, love and a sound mind'.[18] Similarly Otto Shaw, writing a century later, preferred 'a stolid, stable adult to a high-flyer'.[19] The inappropriateness of the 'high-flyer' for a front-line residential care post could be explained by the nature of the care task, suggested in Liz Ward's words quoted above. While he will have more than enough imagination to see how communication between adult and child over the minutiae of daily living, Ward's 'seemingly unimportant incidents', can be used as a vehicle for meeting the child's needs, will he find the repetitive, often dull, daily routine sufficient challenge? How long before he is bored by the work, and how long before his disenchantment is communicated to the child? Some high-flyers might also have difficulty in 'getting down to the level' of the retarded child, finding communication difficult.

The steady, perservering adult, who will stick to the task for many years, gradually refining his skills, is likely to be preferred. Hopefully he will be a patient sympathetic character, clearly perceived by the children to be 'on their side'. He will take their personal problems seriously and be willing to do little extras for them, like mending a treasured broken torch, spending his 'break' untangling a fishing line, searching for a lost toy in the staffroom, giving up time off to take a child to buy a card for his mother's birthday.

His active, emotional and physical involvement will be plain to see. A senior child-care officer commented: 'I like staff who don't stand watching the kids. They are expected to show some initiative, to join in and do things with them.'[20] A visitor to a residential school who spends a few evenings 'on duty' will come to see the differences in care staff. The good will tend to work *among* the children, setting in motion a range of enjoyed activities, surrounding themselves with toys and interesting 'things to do', talking, joking and interacting with the children. At least some members of the team, particularly if working with younger children, will not be afraid of physical contact — pats on backs, comforting arms round shoulders, holding hands, teasingly ruffling hair, helping a young child get dressed, looking at his latest scratches and bruises. These, if not overdone and allowed to develop into over-familiarity, are likely to be signs of a warm, caring person, capable of meeting a child's needs for affection and belongingness. Physical closeness will not prevent the adult from providing the firm, consistent discipline which is also needed.

In contrast the apathetic worker, might sit in the corner of the activities room, newspaper in hand, preserving physical distance between himself and the children, and only intervening when trouble arises. The children soon perceive the emotionally distant member of staff, who *supervises* but does not *participate* in any helpful way, and will sometimes be caught retreating to the sanctuary of the staffroom or seeking the jobs which mean escape from the children. When trouble occurs, he will either abdicate his own responsibility for sorting out the children's problems by passing the buck to the team leader, or perhaps squash any argument in an authoritarian manner, paying little heed to the children's feelings or the causes of the incident. When his official working hours are over, he will abandon the half-finished project whose completion means so much to the child, leaving a frustrated and disgruntled boy for other staff to manage.

He will also waste the opportunities presented in the meeting of basic physical needs. Ward regrets that

Responding to physiological need has sometimes been downgraded as falling outside the social work task. In residential work, however, providing physical care is often the first stage in making the relationship that later becomes the medium for intervention. Using ordinary events, like sharing a meal or helping a person into bed, as opportunities for getting in touch with the 'person inside' is an essential skill for the residential worker.'[21]

Or as Henry Maier reminds us — 'bodily comfort speaketh the loudest'.[22] The good worker will take care to use small opportunities in the daily routine to bring bodily comfort to the child — giving the child an extra, unscheduled hot drink, letting him stay longer than planned in the warm bath, tucking a child in bed last thing at night, or kitting out a child with dry clothes as soon as he has had an 'accident'. Such attention to physical comfort will be noted by the child and might be the required catalyst to a deeper, trusting relationship which can bring about desired changes in behaviour.

The respected staff member will exhibit further qualities. He will be known by the children to be fair, honest, trustworthy, dependable and sympathetic. His firm but not excessively punitive discipline will provide security and clear limit-setting. He will be skilled at defusing potential explosions by means of humour and diversionary tactics. He will not collude with the strong against the weak, as happened in Cottage Six. He will have confronted and outsmarted the most awkward child. An understanding and forgiving attitude will be accompanied by an awareness of children's wiles. He will criticise wrongdoing, possessing the ability, in Morrice's words, 'to tell the truth in love'.[23] Too often, care workers might opt out of this latter responsibility for fear of loss of popularity or desire to stave off trauma as a long day nears its end.

It will be rare for one person to be the embodiment of all the virtues and attitudes sketched above. Most larger establishments will have a wide range of different personalities with contrasting strengths. A balanced care staff will contain a blend of young and old, introvert and extrovert, male and female, 'systems' and 'dyadic' experts. Variety, difficult to achieve in a small, family-group school, can be a positive advantage in helping meet children's shifting preferences and needs. The notion of special 'key worker' can fall down for some children who will look to different staff members to meet different needs. A child might turn to the warm, motherly figure for love and affection; the young PE teacher for challenge on the sports field; the humorous extrovert housefather to jolly him out of his moods; the quiet, serious person to teach him life skills; the strong, authoritarian older man to curb his wilder instincts.

However there will hopefully be one adult with whom the child forms a particularly close relationship, to whom he feels he can turn in moments of trouble, although it could be that this will not be an officially designated 'key worker' or 'named person'. Occasionally it may be the cook or gardener. Otto Shaw reminds us that paper qualifications do not ensure the psychological understanding of maladjustment sometimes possessed by the untrained.[24]

The special person will preferably be a skilled and experienced counsellor — who can exploit shared experiences in the course of daily living for *ad hoc* life-space work and can equally sit down in the privacy of a study and conduct more formal individual sessions. Space does not allow a discussion of the skills required in a counsellor. Readers are referred to advice given by Denis O'Connor[25] on the best use of body gesture, eye contact, touch, facial expression and other non-verbal forms of communication which are the counsellor's props as he helps the child to relax, to open up and to be receptive to advice.

The need to have skilled counsellors on a staff is important for the following basic reasons. Having someone to listen seriously to one's worries about home, about sexual problems, about difficulties in relationships with peers or staff and knowing that the adult is not going to betray confidences, can be a comfort and a boost to the self-esteem of the disturbed and anxious child. It is an avenue for the release of pent-up frustrations and for the receiving of adult assistance. It also presents opportunities for the respected adult to get across to the child the importance of moral values or social skills in which the child may not have realised he is lacking. Counselling can also be used as a branch of 'discipline' — a means of making a child accept an adult decision which he dislikes, or talking a child into apologising to the staff member he has insulted, but this must be a subsidiary function. Counselling should primarily take place for the good of the child rather than the ease of the organisation.

To end this section, we shall turn from adult–child relationships to brief mention of the qualities required in staff if they are to fit comfortably into the overall care team. Many of the virtues identified above will also be required for staff members to get along with and be respected by their colleagues. In addition, they need to be 'professional' in their work. Among other things, this entails loyalty to fellow workers; respect for established school procedures; the upholding of school rules whatever the individual's personal opinion of them; the voicing of criticism openly and honestly through the proper channels of staff meetings or in the presence of staff affected; and the avoidance of collusion with children against colleagues.

As a final comment, the good care worker, while having a quiet determination to improve both his own skills and the effectiveness of the school, will find life easier if he has a patient, even temperament tinged with a sense of humour to help him cope with the unforseeable problems which constantly interrupt the best-thought-out residential routines and obstruct innovation.

HANDLING DAILY ROUTINE

In judging an establishment's standard of child care, attention must be paid to its methods of meeting basic physical needs. What arrangements are made for health care? Are the particular medical needs of individual chilen being met? What clothing is used and how well is it laundered and repaired? Is a sensible balanced diet in adequate quantities provided? Are staff alert to the long-term damage to health caused by the regular eating of additives in common processed 'convenience foods' or, when considering the diets of particular children, the possible links of certain food ingredients to conditions such as hyperactivity or asthma? Is the overweight child being helped to diet?

When considering the quality of provision it is more likely to be a question of *how* rather than *whether* a school meets such physical needs adequately. Is the achievement of 'bodily comfort' an end in itself or is it only a part of providing a richer kind of care, a stepping-stone to each child's higher need fulfilment. Denis O'Connor reminds us that care must be much more than 'the purely mechanistic process of containing people in a state which is clean, tidy, fed and watered, put to sleep and kept warm, and protected fom ever having to think, and act and feel for themselves'.[26] Care workers must try to use the daily routine as a vehicle for social, life-skills and emotional development as well as for the advancement of the child's cognitive skills. Evenings and weekends present an opportunity for educational activity, as suggested in the previous chapter. They should also give the child the chance to develop hobbies, sporting skills and aesthetic interests.

In the following pages we sketch ways, both good and bad, of managing daily routine. While the framework of each day is set by getting up, mealtimes, breaks, lessons, evening activity periods, supper and bedtime, it should be possible to provide a rich and varied lifestyle for each child within this system, which allows for relaxation and play but also helps to develop each pupil's capacity for responsible, independent living. Through tiredness, lack of insight, perhaps of training and sometimes of effort, staff can too easily fail to use the care hours in a way which meets children's higher-level needs.

Getting Up, Meals and Breaktimes

7.15 a.m. in an 'orthodox' school, and a loud bell echoes through the dormitories. Sleepy bodies fall obediently out of bed, take off pyjama tops and stumble to join the lengthening queue at the centrally situated washroom where a staff member makes sure no one escapes the system. His colleague rapidly works his way around the bedrooms turfing sleepy heads out of bed, stripping blankets and sheets to the floor, roundly admonishing anybody daring to steal an extra minute in bed. An atmosphere of sullen resentment prevails — muted bickering out of earshot of staff, silence within their hearing. Clothes are hurriedly pulled on and blankets folded in neat piles at the end of each bed.

The school quickly assembles on hard chairs in neat rows in the hall, watched with an eagle eye by the team leader for signs of fidgeting, boylike banter or any behaviour showing the remotest possibility of developing into naughtiness. 'Jones!' shouts the team leader with the voice of a sergeant-major, 'Stand up and tuck your shirt in!' The boy rises in defeated resignation. 'You always look a mess.' Taking its cue from the staff, the assembled school laugh once more at 'rag and bones' Jones. Then silence reigns for a full ten minutes as the compliant throng await the breakfast bell, and the team leader preens himself on the speed and efficiency of the day's 'get up', and wonders how quickly and quietly he will see them through breakfast.

The school is marched through to the dining room with military precision, and the staff sit down at a separate table for a special breakfast of eggs, bacon, sausage and toast from where they bark at children for poor table manners, too much noise and not finishing their food. Meanwhile the pupils pick at their watery scrambled egg and bread.

The next day, perhaps in the same school, another care team sets to work. At 7.15 a.m. staff gather to read the 'day book' to check on the previous evening's events to see if any boy was showing unusual behaviour. At 7.25, without ringing a bell, the sensitive care worker enters the bedroom containing the children who take longest to dress, turns on the light, draws back the curtains before saying a cheery 'good morning'. He then moves into another room, repeating his opening gambit. Children start to filter to the washbasins, without a queue, without blatant checking by staff. When all rooms have had their curtains drawn, the staff member goes round the rooms again. Most children have now woken; some slowly; some quickly; some require a gentle shake without a rude stripping off of bedcovers. A few who are known to dress quickly are still dozing but this is not seen as an affront to the staff. Others are sitting half awake on the edge of their beds, but they are not chivvied while there are no vacant washbasins for them to use. The care worker finds time for chat and banter to encourage the slow starter or the child who tends to be moody first thing in the morning.

The corridor is definitely noisier than the previous day — there is more laughter and a little horseplay, but the staff member does not feel threatened and even promotes it within the safe limits of the respect and liking the children have for him. One or two boys do attempt to evade their early morning wash, but this does not pass unnoticed and the situation remedied by a quiet word and very little drama or threat of punishment.

Thirty seconds before the community is summoned to breakfast, the slow dressers filter into a cheerful, relaxed atmosphere in the common room. Without any militaristic orders, the community falls silent and listens to the team leader's quiet instructions before the school moves through to the dining room. A houseparent is seen with an arm on the shoulder of the child who had been in aggressive mood the night before, talking quietly. Another, without making a public fuss, quietly draws Peter Jones's attention to his dangling shirt tail. And so to breakfast in an atmosphere of controlled informality, staff mingling with children, sitting at table with them, sharing the same food, gently prompting better table manners and interpersonal skills, softly but effectively reproving the overexcited, noisy child ...

Similar contrasting sketches could be drawn of other 'out-of-lesson' times. In the lunch hour, the caring, sensitive members of staff will allow pupils to play quietly but freely indoors on a cold or wet day; the unfeeling will insist that everybody goes outside, or all watch television in silence when it is raining hard. The caring arrange for children to carry on working on a school project in the classroom or a quiet corner of the living unit. They search out games for children to use on the playground, perhaps joining in or taking the opportunity, while the other children are playing happily, for a quiet chat with the child upset because a promised letter or parcel has failed to arrive from home. The less concerned will put everybody out of doors with an abrupt 'Go out and play' without finding needed equipment or toys. He will only emerge from the staffroom when aroused by a posse of overexcited children who inform him that there has been a fight and two boys have been seen running out of the school gates.

The committed see their task as actively permeating the world of the child, subtly steering pupils towards desired behaviours and values. The less concerned will be content to keep the peace, to glide through meals and breaktimes with the minimum of effort on their part, reacting and dealing with trouble if it arises, but keeping an emotional gap between the children and themselves, failing to create adult–child interactions which further social development.

Evenings

When RSWs are not asked to look after the children at lunchtime, a certain amount of 'time-killing' is understandable in teachers on duty as they seek relaxation after a hard morning and before the renewed pressure of afternoon lessontimes. But no such allowances can be made in the evening care hours.

What shape should after-school routine take? Indeed should there be a regular routine? Some would argue that it makes children institutionalised automatons, incapable of leading an independent lifestyle. Might it not be better if the children chose what they did, when they did it, and how it should be done? Few, however except perhaps for the brightest children, would opt for extreme forms of self-government or a totally *laissez-faire* staff style. Most would agree that evenings should be organised so that a middle course is steered between adult-prompted activity and totally child-centered free time. Children need time to themselves, to relax, to play, to do nothing, or to follow their interests, but too much free time can produce in some children first boredom and then mischief; for others, it means an empty lifestyle of 'hanging around' and an excess of watching television.

Millham *et al*. found children organised in 'breathless activity' from waking until going to sleep happier and more committed to their Approved Schools than children in freer, more informal family-group and therapeutic establishments.[27] Moreover, in these highly organised places, children seemed to absorb more desired adult values, and to fare better in the outside world. So, how important is free time?

Further research is needed, but there seems a need for a degree of structure and imposed activity. Some writers note the emotional support which routines give to many disturbed children, providing a feeling of security, giving children signposts to living and depersonalising orders — a routine is a 'done thing', not decided on the spur of the moment by a member of staff which can be challenged and debated by the awkward child.[28] It is part of the natural order of things, almost built into the bricks and mortar of the school. Of course, routines must be logical, necessary, simple and unfussy. They must not grow into an excess of petty rules and regulations. The wrong routines can be used by less concerned staff to stifle the initiative of pupils, or as an excuse not to grant children's requests which involve risk.

However, within a routine, allowance must be made for free play. Many writers stress the importance of this as the child's natural way of learning. Play is what children *do* and consequently must not be denied to them. It is a chance for experiment, for using imagination, for rehearsing interpersonal skills, for learning from mistakes. For the adjusted child, it is probably better if for some part of the evening the children are left to create their own play, out of adult sight and supervision. But disturbed children might always need adults as 'referees' to prevent games being spoilt by anti-social behaviour, to suggest new activities, to act as role-models, showing children how to take turns, or how to cope with winning or losing games. As the children become better adjusted, this supervision should be withdrawn gradually, giving the chance to test out the maturing child's growing composure, self-control and responsible behaviour.

Time for play will often follow high tea and precede activity periods which commonly occupy the early evening. In schools for average ability children of secondary age there may well be a period of supervised homework, particularly if pupils are studying for national examinations. In many more schools, teachers may play a part in the evening routine once or twice a week, taking activity groups, making use of their particular skills and interests. Sport, outdoor pursuits, art, craft, drama and music will all be popular pastimes, no matter what the school, if organised efficiently and carried out with enthusiasm by capable staff.

In the good school there will also be trips out in the minibus to the local swimming baths, to youth clubs, to special events, to any worthwhile opportunity which will provide new experiences for the children and break down the possible monotony of being cooped up in a boarding school for weeks on end.

The evening activity periods should be an important part of school life. They provide an opportunity for creative and physical activities which in a day school would have to be squashed into an already crowded timetable. If a record is kept of each child's experiences in these areas, thereby ensuring that all pupils take part in them at some time over the school year, it is possible for more of daytime lessons to be devoted to priority education needs, such as extra reading or number work.

A 'guided choice' system of evening activity periods, such as commonly exists in special boarding schools, will enable the educational curriculum to be significantly broadened and directed more specifically at a child's individual special needs. The child 'signs on' for a particular activity for a set period of perhaps half a term. There may be one or two compulsory periods a week designed to meet particular needs, for example remedial PE in the gym for the uncoordinated child, or additional Home Economics tuition for the child approaching leaving. Within a structured system, it is possible to achieve most of this on a voluntary basis. If a particular activity is known to be well directed by the RSW or teacher, it is likely to be popular. Well-run sessions are usually much enjoyed, purposely not as intellectually demanding as formal lessons and permeated with fun. Fears that children will be too tired to benefit from *education* in the *care* hours do not seem to be well founded, although, it must be admitted, there is no empirical evidence to support this statement.

Organised activity periods offer a great opportunity to meet children's higher-level needs. Staff should be conscious of the importance of enhancing pupils' self-image by helping them *achieve*, in whatever area, and to experience repeated success, to motivate them to tackle further confidence-boosting projects of which they can feel proud. They also offer scope for the development of the self-esteem which can spring from successfully participating in group activities, and the rehearsing of improving interpersonal skills. Further, sharing an activity with a child can help a member of staff develop a helpful relationship with him. The activity is a bridge between the two, sometimes acting as a catalyst, enabling the child to 'open up', to talk to or confide in the adult, and to be prepared to listen to the grown-up's advice. 'Doing things together' can be the ideal vehicle for 'life-space counselling'.

It is also very important, particularly for those approaching leaving, that there are times when staff are not present with the children. Older pupils, like teenagers living with their own families, should go out unsupervised into the local community, participating in events, mixing with children who attend day schools. It is essential that they are given responsibility and freedom. On occasion this might be abused, leaving staff with problems to solve which would not have arisen had these children been kept under strict supervision within the school buildings. But only when they have the chance to misbehave will they prove that they can cope with freedom and are making progress towards the independent living which will be required of them when they leave school.

Supper presents a further opportunity for good or bad caring: tepid cocoa and curling-edged sandwiches hastily distributed to the massed children seated silently in rows in the school hall by a housemother anxious to 'get it over' and the washing up done, as the team leader patrols to control noise level or to stop boys kicking the chairs in front; or a small group of children seated one evening in easy chairs in a sitting-room, round a fire with a favourite TV programme on in the background, or the next evening with background music as staff and children mingle in what can be the highlight of the day. The sharing of food, perhaps freshly prepared by some of the group, becomes a symbol of the deep bond which can exist between adults and children. It can act as a catalyst to relaxed and productive group counselling.

Evening washing routines and bedtimes can also be regimented, perfunctory affairs, conducted with great efficiency and speed with little meaningful staff–child interaction, or they can be extended, leisurely times of day, handled with sensitivity. If spread over the second half of the evening, there should be scope for many children to have private baths or leisurely showers, to go up to their rooms at different times to read comics, or listen with headphones to favourite tapes, relaxing unpressured on their beds.

The end of the day can be rigid and unfeeling with a member of staff ringing a bell as soon as he can before hurrying from room to room turning off lights and expecting instant silence from the children; or it can be an extended flexible time, when staff tuck in children, do a girl's hair, help tidy away clothes and toys, read stories, recall the days' events, look forward to the next day, offer advice, discuss little problems, or ask about a child's family. It is likely that, if staff take trouble and spend a little extra time, the children will settle in a happier frame of mind, feeling wanted and liked by staff, and much readier to go to sleep, leaving the adults undisturbed after 'lights out'.

Weekends

In the days before minibuses, videos and weekend leave, it used to be common for staff to dread weekend duties, fearing the long hours and wondering how they would keep bored children out of mischief with reduced staff numbers and limited back-up services. A prayer might be put up for fine weather so that the children would not be cooped up inside in fractious mood. The sound of the bell ringing for the beginning of school on Monday morning would be greeted with a flood of relief. Experienced staff became adept in the use of 'time-killers' — unnecessary clothing checks; repeating bed-making and sweeping-up tasks; making shoe-cleaning a long drawn out Saturday ritual; rehearsing 'disciplines' such as sitting up straight, lining up in classes, walking through from the assembly hall to the dining room in single file without talking. Rarely were children allowed to venture forth from the school grounds, except as part of a 'crocodile' walk, mocked by bystanding local children. Too often, weekends were a time for pointless, sterile routines which did nothing to help children's social or educational development and made little allowance for the natural fun of childhood.

The situation now seems to be much improved. Many boarders go home most if not all weekends. Many more return home at least one weekend per half term, perhaps transported in the school minibuses.

Such home leave probably lessens the inclination to abscond, although this usually happens in the wake of some minor upset or when children are bored and are seeking adventure, rather than through deep homesickness. I remember an incident of a boy from Leeds, another from Newcastle and a third from Lancashire saying they 'missed their mums' and running away together to Glasgow. Absconding could be a constant fear of weekend duty staff working in CHEs or a few schools for the maladjusted with a 'bunking' tradition absorbed by each generation of new pupils. Team leaders would anxiously count heads at each assembly time to identify any absentees before they had time to get too far away from school. The soft, quickly forgiving approach to 'runaways', sometimes advised, is often unsuitable as it can reinforce undesirable behaviour. However, public punishment can create an anti-hero in the eyes of other children. In well-organised, well-staffed schools, even for the most difficult children, absconding is a rare occurrence.

In these establishments, the children who are not going home are likely to experience a relaxed and enjoyable time, receiving more attention from the staff, who are responsible for less children. Similar to weekday care hours, there will be a mixture of free and organised time. Pupils will probably have a 'lie in' and a later breakfast and the opportunity to devote time to their own hobbies, or free play in the school grounds. There will also be the opportunity for longer activities off the premises, such as expeditions to the country or picnics at the seaside; sporting matches against different schools; hill-walking, canoeing, rock-climbing, horse-riding, perhaps outings on a canal barge or other adventure activities commonly on offer in the better schools. Weekends can also be used for overnight Youth Hostelling or camping expeditions.

CONCLUSION

In the care hours, teachers and RSWs should ensure that, in line with needs theory, adequate attention is paid to the individual and, as he grows, changing wants of each child. Merely managing him as part of a large impersonal group and 'warehousing' him by providing adequate food and reasonable comfort is not enough. Physical care should, where possible, be geared to individual need and used as a channel through which the care worker reaches the 'child inside', helping him to feel safety and security in a boarding environment, and inculcating a sense of belonging to the group of children and adults with whom he shares his life. In time most children in boarding schools come to trust the physical and the interlinking emotional support and advice which the school gives to them. For some disturbed children, who might have had disrupted home and day-school lives, coming to a state of *dependency* is a healthy development which should be fostered. As Henry Maier stresses, it is difficult for a child to become independent unless he feels a safe, dependable emotional base to which he can return for support and advice should his experiments in independence go wrong. If he does not feel he has a secure back-up system, made up of understanding people who are concerned about him, he is reluctant to tackle the unfamiliar and his development is likely to become stunted. Maier imagines the three-year-old and, by implication, the older disturbed child saying: 'I want to count on your being with me so that I can comfortably risk doing without you.'[29] Recognition of this feeling, which is common in children, should guide the school's provision for care. Staff should seek the correct balance for each child in his evening programme, allowing for both his need for the support which familiar routine gives him and for his need to try new and unfamiliar experiences, the conquest of which will give him confidence and feelings of self-esteem. For most pupils entering special boarding, the aim should be, first, to guide the child into a trusting dependence upon staff and the school routines, and then, as he settles, matures and is better able to cope with experiments which fail, towards increasing independence.

This process should take place in an atmosphere of controlled informality, in homely surroundings, peopled by concerned and sensitive staff adopting parent-like approaches. This might be less difficult to achieve in a family-group arrangement where only eight or so children live together. In this situation it should also be easier to recognise and meet individual needs or allow for idiosyncrasies. But it is not impossible in other forms of organisation. Whatever the system, rules and discipline should all be present but not encased in a rigid system stifling individuality, reeking of institutionalism and leaving adolescents ill prepared for an independent life when they return home or go to college.

NOTES

1. B. Dockar-Drysdale, *Therapy in Child Care*, Longman, London, 1968.
2. A. Aichhorn, *Wayward Youth*, revised 2nd edn, Imago, London, 1951, p. 150.
3. S.O. Myers, *Where Are They Now?*, RNIB, London, 1975, pp. 4–6.
4. S. Millham, R. Bullock and P. Cherrett, *After Grace, Teeth*, Chaucer, London, 1975.
5. Ibid., p. 93.
6. H. Polsky, *Cottage Six*, Wiley, New York, 1967.
7. M. Wilson and M. Evans, *Education of Disturbed Pupils*, Methuen, London, 1980.
8. D. Stott, *Helping the Maladjusted Child*, Open University Press, Milton Keynes, 1982, p. 38.
9. D. Stanley, 'Northumberland Village Homes: A Historical Perspective', unpublished dissertation, University of Newcastle upon Tyne, 1977.
10. S. Millham, R. Bullock and K. Hosie, *Learning to Care*, Gower, Aldershot, 1980.
11. E.J. Miller and G.V. Gwynne, *A Life Apart*, Tavistock, London, 1972.
12. F. Redl and D. Wineman, *The Aggressive Child*, Free Press, New York, 1957, p. 6.
13. The Education (School Premises) Regulations, SI 909 (1981).
14. D.A. Balla and M.S. Klein, 'Labels for Taxonomies of Environments for Retarded Persons' in H.C. Haywood and J.R. Newbrough, *Living Environments for Developmentally Retarded Persons*, University Park Press, Baltimore, Md, 1981, pp. 3–11.
15. DES, *Boarding Schools for Maladjusted Children*, Building Bulletin no. 27, HMSO, London, 1965; Advisory Council on Child Care (DHSS), *Care and Treatment in a Planned Environment*, HMSO, London, 1970.
16. L. Ward, 'The Social Work Task in Residential Care' in R.G. Walton and D. Elliott (eds), *Residential Care — a Reader in Current Theory and Practice*, Pergamon, Oxford, 1980, p. 25.
17. R. Balbernie, 'Foreword' in Millham *et al.*, *After Grace, Teeth*, p. viii.
18. Reported in J. Carlebach, *Caring for Children in Trouble*, Routledge and Kegan Paul, London, 1966, p. 64.

19. O Shaw, *Maladjusted Boys*, Allen & Unwin, London, 1965, p. 116.
20. M. McCormick, *Away from Home*, Constable, London, 1979, p. 60.
21. Ward, 'The Social Work Task', p. 27.
22. H. Maier, 'Essential Components in Care and Treatment Environments for Children' in F. Ainsworth and L.C. Fulcher, *Group Care for Children*, Tavistock, London, 1981, p. 37.
23. J.K.W. Morrice, 'Basic Concepts: a Critical Review' in R.D. Hinshelwood and N. Manning (eds), *Therapeutic Communities*, Routledge and Kegan Paul, London, 1979.
24. Shaw, *Maladjusted Boys*, p. 115.
25. D. O'Connor, 'Caring and Skills: a Counselling Approach' in J.McG. McMaster (ed.), *Skills in Educational and Social Caring*, Gower, Aldershot, 1982.
26. Ibid., p. 36.
27. Millham *et al.*, *After Grace, Teeth*.
28. The value of routine is stressed in F. Redl, *When We Deal with Children*, Free Press, New York, 1966.
29. Maier, 'Essential Components', p. 30.

7

Caring for the Care Givers

In his blacker moments the despondent head can be forgiven for thinking that staff cause him more problems than pupils. Much of his time
has to be spent talking to teachers and RSWs, soothing ruffled feathers,
seeking compromises which keep conflicting personalities working
together in reasonable harmony, and planning rotas which separate
widely divergent personalities. The apparent cause of such conflict is
often very petty — choice of menu, lost keys, or a child's clothing, rather
than curriculum policy or strategies for the future. Overreaction to
minor problems is common and just one symptom of the stressful and
exhausting nature of working in the goldfish bowl[1] of residential education and care, where nearly everything is done in full view of colleagues
and clients. Mistakes cannot be hidden. There is rarely a private office
door for the teacher or RSW to shut against colleagues or the prob-
lematical children with whom a sometimes ungrateful outside world
expects boarding schools to cope.

Stress can lead to mental and physical exhaustion for all grades of
staff. If care has been taken over administrative arrangements such as
role definition, rotas and systems of communication, such 'burn-out'
can be prevented or at least lessened. Part of good management might
be a supervision system on social services department lines where, as
a matter of course, workers talk to and receive advice from seniors about
their job performance and any worries they might have. A staff-
development programme will also be useful, fostering new teachers'
and RSWs' skills and maintaining the enthusiasm of the experienced.
An underlying malaise may be the RSW's perception that his job is

underpaid and lacks the status and career prospects enjoyed by his teacher colleagues. These topics are discussed in turn before attention is paid to the needs of senior staff. They also need support if they are to remain energetic and interested in their work.

FRUSTRATION AND STRESS OF RESIDENTIAL WORK

Most staffrooms contain one somewhat lazy member who moans about tiredness and how little his hard work is appreciated until he becomes the butt of his colleagues. But there is no doubt that working in residential special schools can be exhausting, frustrating and stressful. If the pupils have learning difficulties, as most do, any education progress may be imperceptible for long periods. Meanwhile parents and perhaps senior staff might expect a teacher to work miracles. Consequently there may be a lack of encouraging feedback. Further, if the children are also disturbed, the worker may have to face the stress of coping with awkward behaviour every day. Even when children are doing well sudden regression to former bad habits can never be ruled out. A slightly bitter point always made to new staff by the dedicated head of a school for disturbed slow learners, after thirty years in the work was: 'The one thing you can rely on these children to do, is to let you down.'[2]

Even when such children are not being naughty or aggressive, the lifestyle can be worrying and debilitating. Take a sunny Sunday lunch-hour when all the children are apparently playing peacefully out of doors, and the staff are briefly relaxing in the staffroom before afternoon activities begin. There may be a sudden rush of footsteps and loud knocking on the door before breathless kids excitedly announce, 'George has fallen from the top of the big beech tree. He can't move, sir!' Behind a calm exterior, the team leader's mind races. Has he broken his neck? Or his back? Perhaps only a wrist and he has fainted. As he walks out of the staffroom, the rest of his team share his anguish. He recalls the boy killed ten years ago who disobeyed school rules at school camp and fell off an 'out of bounds' cliff and drowned ... telling the parents ... the inquest ... questions about the school in the press ... Or the boy at the nearby school who was run over on a road race. As he goes out of the school building, he is greeted by George, bruised and a little tearful but intact. A happy outcome this time, but will the next occasion end as happily? Should that beech tree be put out of bounds? Should all tree climbing be banned? Should staff be watching all children every moment of the day? If he 'plays safe', as half his team now want him to, he knows he will be providing a sterile, institutionalised form of care which is not in the children's long-term interests and which might produce bored and fractious children 'playing up' junior members of staff.

A thoughtful child in a children's home reflected:

> The staff in our place are a great bunch really. They've got a 24 hour job. And who would want to live with us 24 hours a day? One night they might get some peace, but one night I remember, my little brother fell out of bed and cracked his head. He split all his head open and he was bleeding everywhere. So we bombs up the stairs and gets the staff up. And they got up and took him to hospital. That is not much privacy.[3]

Similarly, in boarding schools, worry related to the possibility of accidents will affect even the most junior member of staff. He might be in charge of a group containing a haemophiliac who cuts himself, or an epileptic who has a *grand mal* fit. All he can do is watch in helpless but distressing sympathy. Five minutes later the same member of staff will be expected to be bouncy, cheerful, playing games with other children. Within a quarter of an hour, he could be facing hostility and aggression from disobedient teenagers when intervening to stop a fight or working through a tangle of deceit trying to establish who has stolen a boy's watch.

Not surprisingly, many care workers rapidly discover that the lifestyle is not for them. Martha Mattingly, in her excellent description of the stresses facing the RSW, wrote of the fast-dissipating enthusiasm of the new care worker:

> The idealism and dedication which characterize the decision to engage in caring work are severely challenged by numerous physical and psychological assaults on wellbeing and self-esteem. Upon entering the field, workers usually perceive themselves as concerned and helpful persons whom clients and society will value. By way of contrast, workers are confronted by assaultive youth, messy and aggressive children, and ungrateful families. The nobility of caring work turns out to be a myth. Successful workers develop a personal durability as they integrate the idealistic view of caring for children with the everyday realities. However, no matter how skilled and sophisticated the worker, a kick in the shins, broken glasses, an insult, and a child's lack of progress are all assaults on self-esteem which threaten workers' perceptions of their helping ability.[4]

Many authors comment on the rapid staff turnover experienced in some residential establishments. Further, it has been suggested that it tends to be the over-authoritarian who stay for prolonged periods in the work.[5] This is backed up by the child in the children's home who remarked: 'Some of the good staff leave because they just need a break. They have got to have a break, like we have got to have a break. Because ten to one the good staff are more popular, and the more it takes out of them.'[6] However there are many schools, even for the most disturbed, where staff turnover is not high, where the 'walking wounded' are healed and motivation restored. With sensitive and skilled leadership, new and experienced staff can be helped to cope with trauma, to develop the emotional reserves needed to find long-term fulfilment in residential work.

FIGHTING 'BURN-OUT'

How do you recognise the worker who is 'burning out'? In the early stages, a keen and probably very capable staff member starts feeling discontented with his work. He might feel inadequate, and start to question his effectiveness in his job. He might seek excessive reassurance from senior staff, constantly apologising when there is no need. Alternatively his behaviour might become rigid, his mind closed to new ideas, his tolerance for those about him limited. He may indulge in 'negative labelling' of children and colleagues. He may cease to trust the adults around him, believing the only way to do a job properly is to do it himself. He might enter into collusive relationships with a small clique of colleagues, increasingly enjoying the trials and tribulations of other staff, perhaps adopting petty 'point-scoring' attitudes. At the same time, he will become obsessive about work, enjoying the martyrdom of volunteering for extra duties, staying behind unnecessarily when duties are over, finding it impossible to lead a social life unconnected with the school. There may be recourse to overeating, excessive coffee or alcohol consumption or use of tranquillisers leading to worse physical health, irregular sleep and increased mental stress. He may be unaware of needs theory in relation to his own life, caught in a worsening cycle, leading to the edge of paranoia and breakdown. Too many workers reach this extreme situation, by which time they are heavily defensive and averse to genuine efforts to relieve their stress by advice or offers of help.

It is probably less common for care workers to reach this state today than it was some years ago, when staff were required to work exhausting duty systems, for example, four complete days on followed by four days off, or rotating systems which precluded participation in all regular social activities. Nowadays, work rotas will give adequate time off; in recent years, the required working week has shortened considerably, and staffing ratios have improved, allowing more cover in times of sickness, while holiday entitlements have also improved for RSWs.

However, to offset this trend, the children might be more difficult. Furthermore, a dedicated worker might still indulge in a noble but extreme devotion to his work, insisting on doing extra projects, having children in his own home when off duty, giving up his holidays to take pupils on trips, refusing to accept offers of help from other staff. If he does this, he is likely to fall increasingly into bad habits. A correct balance has to be struck between commitment and a masochism which will in time affect the worker's effectiveness. The ability to 'switch off' from work, to seek physical and mental refreshment through hobbies or a social life, must be refound if it has been lost. Time off should guarantee peace and quiet undisturbed by work worries, and the worker should have sufficient energy left to seek self-fulfilment through channels unrelated to his routine work.

To lessen 'burn-out' the head and his senior colleagues who plan the organisation of the school should take trouble to see that staff are able to use their off-duty hours in these ways. While voluntary extra commitment to the children is to be welcomed and warmly encouraged in moderation, senior staff should be aware of the strains that can be placed on a person who feels morally obliged to do more than is compatible with meeting the demands of his own family life. Staff can be caught between being expected by senior staff, though not obliged, to do extra work and matching the expectations of an incomprehending spouse, who sees family life restricted and disrupted by the care worker's devotion to his work.

Divided loyalties may be accentuated where a worker has to live on site, perhaps in a small flat in the middle of the school. A wife may not understand how a RSW feels obliged to answer the request of a colleague on duty asking for help in locating a lost key. The constant intrusion of children's voices, perhaps their arguments or swearing, into his own young child's bedroom at night will lead to further friction, and drive the off-duty RSW to venture out of his flat to play an active part in the control of the children. It may be difficult for 'living-in' staff to receive visitors, or to make private telephone calls. Upset pupils may expect counselling and comfort, making no distinction between on-duty and off-duty periods. In short, there might be little escape from the stresses of normal working hours. Governing bodies and senior staff are increasingly recognising the need for careful physical planning of staff flats so that privacy is better protected.

They are also encouraging staff to buy or rent their own property off site and to 'sleep in' on their duty nights. Schools following this practice might well have less staff turnover and a more relaxed, better-motivated staff. People in their thirties or forties will be more attracted to the work. Resident housestaff do tend to be young single people whose verve sometimes does not compensate for lack of the life experience which can be so helpful in earning the respect of pupils.

Where long-stay staff are residential, there is also a danger that their outlook will become inward-looking, and the standards they expect of the children will become remote from those of the world outside. Living out often helps adults to preserve a broader, more balanced perspective on life. Away from school, the day's crises diminish in importance — feelings of dismay or contempt for the methods of colleagues dissipate and a more charitable attitude re-emerges.

Managing the interpersonal problems of staff is likely to be one of the head's most daunting tasks. Personality clashes which occur within a tightly knit care team will lessen a team's effectiveness with pupils. Such clashes will also place great stress on the characters involved as they try to present a professional front to the pupils and to discuss differences in a civilised manner out of their hearing. Occasionally there may be a public outburst followed by guilt feelings causing further stress. Some may release pent-up feelings by quiet collusion with pupils against the other member of staff. They know this to be wrong, but are unable to stop themselves. If the school is a small family-group establishment, such conflict can be devastating to the smooth running and effectiveness of the institution. In the larger school senior staff have more scope for splitting conflicting personalities, placing them on different teams, putting physical and emotional space between them.

Committed heads and deputies will spend hours working on duty rotas. This will happen many weeks in advance of the new term to give staff time to plan their social life and adjust to redefined roles. Senior staff will think through the different permutations, aiming for the happiest blend of personalities while trying to avoid stagnation. Some workers may become so used to the methods of long-standing colleagues that they fail to notice that they are developing bad staff-orientated practices. They become blind to the new ideas and happier atmosphere existing in different parts of the organisation. Having tactfully discussed the situation with the personalities involved, the head should seek to move those who are stagnating to a different team. It might be presented as a necessary swop to allow a young member of staff to widen his experience.

Development of the newcomer must also be a duty of senior staff. First, a careful induction period should take place, in which the novice works alongside experienced people, observing methods, learning the 'ins and outs' of the organisation. There should be experienced staff on hand with whom the novice can discuss problems. As he gains experience and shows increasing competence his role needs to be redefined and more responsibilities given to provide challenge and maintain motivation.

Senior staff will cultivate the inexperienced and burgeoning, but should also tend the tired and experienced whose performance may be slipping. It may be that after many years' excellent work with the older, most challenging children, a jaded teacher will be happier transferring to a less stressful position working with younger pupils. The sensitive antennae of the good head will be alert to such needs and, in the process of observing staff at work, will look out for regressions, searching for the best ways to use a person's strengths.

Good management means involving staff as much as possible in contributing to the planning of school life. Residential staff generally prefer a democratic but positive leader who recognises their right to a say in the framing of their own working lives, who lets them know clearly what is expected of them, and keeps them informed well in advance of any plans which affect them. However, an autocrat is better than a leader who lets things drift, gives little clear guidance, adopts an *ad hoc* approach which can cause havoc to staff's daily routine and perhaps social lives, thereby increasing stress.

Good communication is one of the most difficult management goals to achieve in a boarding school with a large staff. Senior staff must make every effort to keep teachers and RSWs informed of plans, altered routine, information from children's families or county hall. Yet staff should recognise the difficulties faced by heads and deputies. Senior staff cannot be expected to spoon-feed every member of staff with every titbit of information. Teachers and RSWs must make the effort to keep themselves informed by reading reports, looking at notices and talking to colleagues.

SUPPORT THROUGH 'SUPERVISION'

Unwarranted criticism of heads and deputies can be lessened by a well-established staff-supervision system. Informal chats snatched during the lunch hour or long outpourings over supper after an evening duty ends have their place and senior staff should use these methods to support staff.

Similarly, they will probably arrange counselling sessions *after* a crisis has occurred, perhaps when faulty attitudes or approaches to care have already damaged a child. But these are not felt to be enough by social services departments for field workers, each of whom will have a supervisor — a senior of proven ability who is usually not the person's line manager. One-to-one meetings will be arranged at regular intervals whose frequency will be determined by the experience and need of the supervisee. Such sessions can be hurried interrupted affairs of little value but, if accorded the importance they deserve, they can be a useful method of helping staff development, and of lessening pent-up stress. While preserving confidentiality, the supervisor can act as advocate on the supervisee's behalf, helping to resolve role conflict and air genuine grievances to the line manager, often defusing potentially explosive situations. Tactful, constructive criticism of the worker's attitudes and performance will also have a place. If nothing else, the harrassed worker has someone to talk to without feeling that by talking he is affecting his chances of promotion.[7]

The need for the line manager not to be the supervisor may be overstated. It is unlikely that the sensitive head or deputy will not already have a clear idea of what a staff member thinks, and will have definite notions of a person's potential for further responsibility. There can be few secrets in such establishments. Also there may be a lack of senior staff who are not part of the line management. So a supervisor might have to be a deputy or even the head, if a teacher or RSW relates well to him. Staff who fear that such a system would be used merely to criticise and judge them might be pleasantly surprised by the praise and genuine appreciation which comes their way. And senior staff, who tend to be tight-lipped with compliments, would do well to remember that praise stimulates desired learning rather than making the worker complacent.

STAFF DEVELOPMENT

A care worker might seek further learning by asking to attend a full-time course. This notion might be greeted by his head with trepidation if the latter has seen others follow traditional courses, learn few new skills, return imbued with ideas which cannot be realised quickly in their place of work, and become more disenchanted with their employment. One study found workers returning from social work courses depressed, bored and anomic.[8] Further, existing social work courses, in particular most versions of the CQSW, devote insufficient time to residential work with children, and teachers on the CSS course may not have a close knowledge of the workings of boarding schools run by LEAs.

Alan Jacka, in his short history of the National Children's Home, suggested: 'If you want the right staff you must grow them yourselves.'[9] Millham *et al.* agree that, for some workers at least, part-time, work-place-based training, planned and devised by senior staff, a trusted psychologist or other consultant, is more appealing. A student remains in touch with his colleagues and pupils. If this is backed up with some of the relevant modern distance-learning courses evolved by the Open University, a powerful method of increasing awareness and knowledge exists. Where this leads to nationally recognised qualifications the popularity of such training is increased.

Modern video technology should be more widely used for staff development. It is a practical way of bringing the methods and experience of other special schools into sometimes insular boarding establishments. Video could also be used more widely for filming practitioners in action with pupils or in role-play with fellow adult students. Staff can view their own actual performance, subject it to detailed transactional analysis, and see their strengths and weaknesses. The nervous student could view the videotape in private if he fears his self-esteem is threatened by public exposure of his failings. Senior staff planning such work should study the work of John McMaster[10] for advice on how to maximise the benefits of such skills-based training. His account tells of the initial reservations of students being overcome. Students on courses for example at the Ulster Polytechnic and at Newcastle University came to value such 'microteaching', appreciating the clear feedback which video gave. Experience suggests that skill developed in this manner did transfer to day-to-day work with children and boosted the former student's self-esteem.

IS A BETTER DEAL FOR RSWs POSSIBLE?

The low status and marginality commonly felt by RSWs has been noted in various publications over the last twenty years.[11] Too often they have found themselves allocated the worst hours of work with inadequate support from senior staff and very poor conditions of service in comparison with teachers. Even an experienced and skilled senior RSW will find himself earning considerably less money than a junior and perhaps indifferent teacher. All his working hours may fall in the evenings or weekends while the less committed teacher only seems to work from nine to four, Monday to Friday. He may only receive five or six weeks' holiday a year compared to the teacher's fourteen weeks. Yet he will be coping with the same difficult children, and perhaps at the same time be asked to perform menial domestic tasks felt to be below the dignity of many teachers, such as cooking and housework, not as part of the education of the children, but in place of cleaners and other domestic assistants. Such conditions of service, often diverging considerably from formal job descriptions, probably explain the rapid turnover of RSWs noted by various authors.

The Warnock Report was conscious of this situation and felt that the setting up of a specialist course for RSWs in boarding schools (other than existing CCETSW courses whose content, as has already been noted, was not felt to be sufficiently relevant for some boarding-school workers) might be of help, giving RSWs a firm base of professional knowledge.[12] This might better equip them for senior positions of responsibility. It also wanted a clearly defined career structure, making the suggestion that a post at deputy head level in charge of all child-care arrangements[13] should be open to trained child-care staff. More schools have perhaps adopted this practice by now.

However, the stumbling block of low salaries remains. While conditions of service have improved considerably, given the tight financial restrictions under which boarding schools operate, it has not been possible to bring salary scales up to a level attractive enough to entice many high-quality staff. This may have happened in CHEs; but the resulting escalation of costs was probably the biggest factor in the closing down of a large proportion of these schools and the consequent unemployment of many of the staff. In the present imperfect world, some schools therefore prefer to keep relatively well-paid teachers in charge of care arrangements, and to employ RSWs at a more junior level under the teacher's command. In practice, given the greater difficulties of attracting RSWs of managerial quality, this probably makes for the smoother running of their schools, but does nothing to ease the RSWs' feelings of marginality. If such teachers underwent child-care training, as recommended by the Warnock Committee,[14] they might be more happily accepted in this role.

Where, in practice, RSWs, despite their valuable work, are consigned to junior positions, senior staff can mitigate their feelings of malaise by arranging rotas so that teachers are *seen* to share the burden of weekend and evening work, and are not excused from less attractive care responsibilities. They might also be able to provide longer holidays for RSWs who are prepared, like the teachers helping with evening duties, to work extra hours in termtime.

No head would deny promotion over teachers to the qualified RSW of proven all-round ability. Where such people are found in boarding schools, they richly deserve a salary level and conditions of service commensurate with that given to teaching staff.

SENIOR STAFF NEEDS

Too much can be required of senior staff in boarding schools. The head has to fill a variety of stressful roles including those of diplomat and emissary to the outside world; efficient administrator; counsellor to parents, staff and pupils; disciplinarian; strategic planner; evaluator; resource getter; teacher of children; staff developer; RSW; building inspector; safety officer; handyman and probably many others. His time off will be even less sacred than that of his staff. His family could be more neglected and his privacy limited as he will probably live on site. He will be expected to be available for much of the holidays. Whatever his talents, he could be a victim of at least partial burn-out after a few years in his post. It is essential that he receives as much help as possible from his deputies, governing body and hopefully a sympathetic, supportive staff. His is an isolated, highly responsible post and he is more likely to perceive hostility and criticism from those he governs than the praise he has earned. He, too, needs a sympathetic ear to bend on a regular basis — someone to advise and encourage, someone on whom to sound out his plans, someone to criticise him in a non-judgmental manner. A trusted deputy might partly fulfil this role, as might an LEA adviser or consultant psychologist who could call regularly for this purpose. The non-teaching director of the independent school can also be a confidant and adviser, as perhaps can an active governor or trustee of a non-maintained school.

The good head will put himself out on behalf of his assistant staff, covering illness, sorting out their problems, rearranging duties to allow for special occasions, respecting their time off. In return, assistant staff should repay the head by trying not to invade his privacy, by offering to relieve him of the routine burden when he is unwell, by not expecting instant attention when they can see that he is working under pressure.

Similarly, the county hall or the independent proprietor should help the head by taking seriously problems which, away from the school, might not seem important. The broken boiler or minibus awaiting repair will be causing havoc to school life. Sanctioning the necessary work should not be put off until after the weekend. Correspondence should be dealt with promptly.

It is essential for the well-being of a residential school that senior staff are supported efficiently and helped to stay on top of their jobs in good physical and mental health. Without energetic and clear leadership from a well-motivated head, a school will quickly deteriorate. If the head is burning out, developing habits of negative labelling, exhibiting a pessimistic, fatalistic view of residential work, perhaps hiding behind a welter of non-essential paperwork instead of making decisions, and treating pupils and staff in an increasingly authoritarian and disrespectful manner, he should no longer be in post. If he has been allowed to reach this state, the managing body must find ways of replacing him however difficult and painful this might be. Too often local authorities avoid this responsibility, waiting too long for a distant retirement date or praying that the person actually breaks down and has to retire. Of late, early retirement has eased the situation but perhaps should be used more often. Transfer to another post or dismissal should not be considered impossible options when the welfare of already handicapped children is at stake, and the stress of working under an inadequate head is affecting the morale and perhaps the health of so many staff. Extreme measures should be accompanied by generous compensation if a head, as is often the case, has given many years' good service. Fixed-term contracts and probationary periods for novice heads might be other safeguards which could be used more frequently. Turning a blind eye to this problem has probably done more harm to the quality of residential special education than most other factors.

NOTES

1. This image was suggested by Henry Maier.
2. T.L. Cole, personal communication, 1974.
3. R. Page and G. Clark (eds), *Who Cares: Young People in Care Speak Out*, National Children's Bureau, 1977, p. 22.
4. M.A. Mattingley, 'Occupational Stress for Group Care Personnel' in F. Ainsworth and L. Fulcher (eds), *Group Care for Children*, Tavistock, London, 1981, p. 154.
5. J. Berry, *Daily Experience in Residential Life*, Routledge and Kegan Paul, London, 1975, p. 63.
6. Page and Clark, *Who Cares*, p. 22.
7. D.E. Pettes, *Staff and Student Supervision*, George Allen & Unwin, London, 1979.
8. S. Millham, R. Bullock and K. Hosie, *Learning to Care*, Gower, Aldershot, 1980.
9. A. Jacka, *The Story of the Children's Home*, National Children's Home, London, 1969, p. 14.
10. J.McG. McMaster, 'Training: a Skills Approach' in McMaster (ed.), *Skills in Educational and Social Caring*, Gower, Aldershot, 1982, pp. 37–66.
11. Millham *et al.*, *Learning to Care*, p. 17.
12. Committee of Enquiry into the Education of Handicapped Children and Young People, *Special Educational Needs* (Warnock Report), Cmnd. 7212, HMSO, London, 1978, para. 14.36, p. 275.
13. Ibid., para. 14.37, pp. 275–6.
14. Ibid., para. 14.36, p. 275.

8

In Partnership with the Family

Some years ago, a teacher in an American residential school for the deaf is reported to have said about his pupils: 'now that they're here, these children are ours, and we don't want the parents to interfere.'[1] Hopefully, this attitude no longer persists even for the minority of families where there might be a feeling of relief that the child no longer has to be cared for at home, accompanied by an attitude of 'out of sight, out of mind'. The majority of children in residential schools will come from the 'mendable families' described in Chapter 2 or from supportive households not beset with problems. These parents have every right to be kept fully informed and to play an active part in the child's schooling, and it is in the youngster's interests that they do. Children perform better socially and educationally when their parents take a keen and continuing interest in their development.

Teachers' open expression of a desire to exclude parents from their children's education might now be rare, but obstacles might still be placed in the way of the parent wishing to be actively involved. Busy staff might not like to see daily routines disturbed, however minimally, by visitors. They may feel hampered when watched at work by parents. These reasons probably explain the perception of the mother of a deaf child who said about her four-year-old deaf child's school: 'They say 'Come whenever you like', but you never feel really that you're welcome, you're bound to be interrupting something.'[2] Where parents feel they are getting in the way, they tend to retreat from attempts to keep themselves involved in their child's school life. Meanwhile their incomprehending child might feel rejected.

Parents are left feeling helpless and subject to persistent worry caused by their ignorance of what their child is doing, how he is being looked after and who is caring for him. Up to the moment of his entry into residential education, they had been responsible for him all day every day. They may have had difficulty and admitted that they needed the help offered by boarding placement, but they had so far coped with their child with only limited help from outsiders. Suddenly, the past is made irrelevant and a new strategy is adopted in which there is no place for the parent ... until the next holidays. Then, without any communication from the school about what has happened in the previous term and without means of contacting the school staff now away on holiday, the parent is again confronted by the task of looking after his child, who is perhaps altered and more distrustful because of his absence from home.

This same disjointed procedure may continue for years. The child lives two separate lives, with two sets of adults who hardly communicate and have little understanding of each other. Time passes, the child reaches sixteen and is thrust back with little preparation for fifty-two weeks a year into his family. Nothing further is heard from the school.

Hopefully, this oversimplified scenario rarely exists, but some residential schools should make much greater efforts to bridge the gap between home and school. In the following pages, suggestions will be made for establishing a close and helpful partnership between staff and parents.

PREPARING FOR A CHILD'S ENTRY INTO BOARDING SCHOOL

The seeds of a trusting partnership should be sown before a pupil goes to board. The first knowledge a parent may gain of a school could be given in the school's prospectus. The psychologist or day-school head should have copies of this, ready to give to parents. LEAs now have a legal duty to ensure that detailed information describing the curriculum and the kind of provision made is produced by each of its schools[3] and is available to parents. It does not cost a fortune to produce an attractive document illustrated with pictures, perhaps with a flap in the back cover for the inclusion of information which can date and needs replacing quickly. It is important that parents should see at an early stage that the boarding school is not the grim, Victorian institution, prison or mental hospital they may have imagined. Carefully prepared material, free of jargon, can help to dispel these fears.

The next stage is to arrange a visit to the school, to let the family 'interview' the school staff, as well as for the head and his senior colleagues to see if the child is suitable for admission. If parents find transport difficult, or are nervous of going to a strange new place, local authority officers, whether from the education or social services, must make every effort to provide physical and moral assistance to achieve the all-important first face-to-face encounter between family and school staff. Telephone calls and letters are a poor substitute for such meetings. Without actually going to the school and getting to know the staff, parents might well harbour suspicions, resentments and fears. Similarly, staff who do not know a child's parents may indulge in unwarranted negative labelling and blaming of parents.

This preliminary visit must not be a perfunctory affair, squashed into a head's busy schedule. Creating a favourable first impression is most important. Time and care must be devoted to it, appropriate to the occasion. The family should be given a warm welcome by staff who have done their homework. It is rude and uncaring for professionals to be thumbing surreptitiously through a child's records in the presence of the family, or not remembering his mother's new surname if she has remarried. Unrealistic promises should not be made of miraculous progress and rapid reintegration. Only honesty and realism are likely to win the family's lasting trust.

To allow more open discussion it is often sensible for the child to go out to play with other pupils. While the child's view should be heard and he should feel that he is respected in his own right, it can be unnecessarily painful for a child to sit through a discussion of the family's problems.

If possible, both child and parent should be introduced to the staff who will be teaching and caring for the child. Perhaps the mother could spend a few minutes in the teacher's class. She should also be given a full and uncensored tour of the school facilities, wherever possible seeing children use them. More often than not, in a well-established school, she will be pleasantly surprised by the happiness and enthusiasm of the children, who will be proud to show visitors what they are doing, or where they sleep, or tell them about the enjoyable activities arranged in the evening care hours. Eating lunch in the same room as the children can be another reassuring experience for the apprehensive mother. Here she should see that the children will be physically well cared for. She should also see the relaxed, caring relationship which will exist between staff and children sitting together.

There will be too much to absorb in a few hours, so it is often helpful for this first visit to be followed up by the head or school social worker's ringing the parent a few days later to see if there are any further questions. If a parent's group exists or there is a national society of which the parent is not a member, school staff could help the mother to make contact with these.

It is also important for at least one member of the school staff to pay a visit to the family home, to gain an impression of their lifestyle and an understanding of the problems besetting the family. It could well be that the mother will feel freer and more confident talking in her own home than in the strange surroundings of the school. If school staff have knowledge of the home, the child's locality and an acquaintance with the pupil's brothers and sisters and even the pet dog, it can help towards the early establishment of the desired relaxed and trusting relationship between school and family.

A SENSITIVE INDUCTION

In most boarding schools attention will be paid to helping a new child 'settle in', but his parents may also need assistance in adjusting to a new lifestyle without their child. A mother may be suddenly freed from stress and physical exhaustion but a painful void may be left. Guilt feelings about having rejected her child might be made worse by official emphasis on the advantages of non-residential care. In addition, the emotional pain caused by the parting can be aggravated if the parent feels ill informed about the quality of the care her child is receiving, or if she does not yet trust the staff of the boarding school. Susan Gregory records the words of the mother of a five-year-old child with hearing impairment, reflecting on the trauma of leaving her young child for the first time in a boarding school:

> I stayed the first day, I put him to bed at night, I stayed in the hotel opposite, put him to bed myself at night. But the Headmaster wouldn't let me stay the next day, and I badly wanted to, just to see the routine and what they did but he said 'No, ten o'clock's long enough'. So I went and said good-bye to him at ten o'cloock. It was terrible. I'd love to go. I really would. For a whole week.[4]

This school had gone to some lengths to ease the mother's pains at parting. Less sensitive establishments may insist on a brisk handover of the child in the visitors' reception room, without even showing the mother where the child will be sleeping. But the follow-up seems to have been lacking. Was she encouraged to ring up and speak to the head and her child the day after he started at the school? Why was not she invited to come and stay at the school overnight in the parents' flat, or if this facility is lacking, in the school sick-room (often a much under-used facility) a few weeks later? In this way she would see the school's routine and how her child was settling in.

Of course, a balance has to be struck; some parents can be unrealistic about the amount of time it is fair to expect staff to devote to them. Only one or two parents can successfully mingle with school life at a time, if the smooth running of the school is not to be disturbed or other children neglected. However, schools must do what they can to allay parental fears, particularly for the mothers of new pupils, and usually the best way to do this is to give parents as free a rein as possible in a school for the duration of their visit. This is likely to be more convincing than counselling sessions from the head in a quiet room, cocooned from the reality of daily life at the school. However, these too have an important place in building up trust.

KEEPING IN TOUCH THROUGHOUT THE CHILD'S STAY

Children in special boarding schools need frequent letters, phone calls and parcels from home to let them know that they remain in their family's thoughts, that the bond of affection between parent and child has not been weakened by the child's absence. Further, for them to prosper educationally, they need to know that their parents or other significant adults in their lives continue to take a keen interest in their education, sharing their classroom triumphs and tribulations. When a child boards many miles from his home and only sees his family intermittently, it is difficult for him to assess whether this necessary interest exists or not. If the school does not involve the families in the educational process, the parents, while continuing to miss their child, might lose interest in the specifics of his educational programme. The boarding child will not be able to take home a piece of good classroom work at the end of the day to show his mother. Opportunities for quick positive feedback from parents will be more limited and because of this the child's motivation in class might be dampened. Residential school staff must be aware of this problem. Positive parental feedback is very important to the child. Consequently teachers must do all they can to keep the parents genuinely involved, enabling and encouraging them to communicate their interest in their child.

Some schools will remember this for the new child and his family but then, if the child is reasonably settled and there is no adverse feedback from the home, cease to cultivate the relationship with the parents. The latter might be restricted to the occasional bland school report and nothing more. Fears and doubts may build up of which the school has no inkling; new factors may complicate the home situation, affecting the child's emotional or social behaviour. All may appear calm until suddenly a crisis occurs for which the school staff is unprepared. A child might suddenly 'kick over the traces'. The school may respond with disciplinary measures which are reported in exaggerated and distorted form by the child to his parents on his return home. Just as the teaching and care staff go away for their own holidays, an angry mother might arrive unannounced at the school. With difficulty, after confronting the caretaker and the cook, she locates the head. She accuses him and the rest of his staff of various kinds of malpractice and threatens to take her child away and report the school to the LEA.

Such situations should rarely arise if the school does its job properly. If staff take the trouble to keep in regular contact with the child's family, they will be aware of pending trouble. Forewarned, they may able to avert the disturbed child's explosion at school. Even if this happens, they should quickly get in touch with the mother to inform her of events and hopefully to elicit her support for any disciplinary action felt necessary. More often than not, if parents are apprised of the facts and if trusting the staff involved, they will give the necessary support. Most will also know that the staff are being responsible and truthful so their son's perhaps embroidered accusations should not be taken seriously. In the right relationship, if the parent were worried she would feel free to ring up the headteacher or other member of staff, perhaps the child's keyworker or 'named person', who keeps in regular touch with her and with whom she has a good relationship, before she became so 'worked up' that she felt she had to pay an emergency visit to the school.

The child could have taken home examples of good classroom work at weekends to show to his parents, along with a praising note from his teacher. The latter could have kept in touch by phone, or kept a home-school diary through which staff and parents keep in touch about the child, and try to co-ordinate their approach to him. The head could have insisted on the writing of more regular and more helpful reports, designed for the parents rather than for the professionals who instigated the placement.

INVOLVING PARENTS IN PROGRAMME PLANNING AND EXECUTION

Public Law 94-142 in the United States and the 1981 Education Act in England both decree that parents should be much more involved in the education of their children, and that their views must be taken seriously by professionals. Meanwhile evidence accumulates that parents *can* make a positive contribution to their children's learning, for example, helping their reading development or carrying out life-skills programmes designed in conjunction with school staff. It is therefore disappointing that recent authors such as Steven Apter still feel it necessary to berate teachers and other trained personnel for continuing to cultivate 'the myth of powerlessness',[5] convincing parents that only the professionals have the answers to children's problems and that, consequently, programme planning should be left to them. Similarly, Young and Tyre talk of the 'aura of mystique and of esoteric and recondite practices'[6] used by educators to patronise the parent worried about his child's lack of progress. Parents must be encouraged to contribute to both the planning and (where relevant) to the execution of their children's individual programme.

As a minimum, parents must attend the annual review likely to be held at the residential school. They should be given plenty of warning of the planned date, and if it is impossible for them to make it on that day, an alternative should be arranged. If transport is difficult, the authority's psychologist or other education or social work office representative could give the family a lift. Failing that, in establishments where there is a school car this could be despatched to fetch them, or at least transport arranged from the railway or bus station. On arrival at the school, as for the initial interview, the staff should be ready to devote time and effort to the parents. It is not adequate for the review to be squeezed in to a fifteen-minute schedule on a day when half a dozen other families are also present at the school. The parents have a right to spend some hours in the school, perhaps a little of it spent in class observing their child at work. Time might also be spent in informal interaction with the staff. More may be gleaned before and after the formal meeting than during it as staff and parents relax over a cup of coffee or chat over lunch.

The review meeting itself should be a mixture of reporting on the past months and looking ahead to the future. Parents must be allowed full opportunity to give their interpretation of recent events and how they feel their child is performing. Is there a wide discrepancy between the school staff's account and the parent's own feelings? If so, how can this be explained? Parents commonly complain that special schools set too low academic targets for their pupils. Teachers must come to this meeting prepared to describe in detail what a child is doing in class and why he is doing it, able to convince the doubting parent. Staff and parents should also give a full report on social and emotional development, comparing notes on the child's behaviour in the school and his home setting.

The review should lead to a clear plan for the next few months. Parents should have a good understanding of what the staff are doing with their child, hopefully with confidence in their ability reinforced. They should also have agreed their own contribution. How are the skills which the child is acquiring at school to be transferred to the home environment? Are there any programmes which the parents can usefully carry out as an extension of their child's schoolwork at weekends and in the holidays.

It is often sensible for a teacher or the school social worker to follow up the annual review with a visit shortly afterwards to the child's family. He should take along a copy of the written report which resulted from the review. In the child's home, the staff member and parent can go through the report, checking to see that what was written was understood by the parents and was a true account of the parents' own views. Were there other matters which the parent wished to raise but felt reluctant to do so in the presence of so many people or perhaps in the presence of a particular member of the school's staff of whom he was suspicious? After reflecting on the promises a parent had made at the review, did he feel that he could carry out the planned home programme? Together, the staff member and parent could work out the practical details of the new scheme in the actual environment in which it was to take place, thinking of the plans, ensuring that the parent has the means to see the programme through.

It has been claimed that letters and chats to parents are inadequate ways of getting parents to ensure the transfer of new skills from school to home.[7] A more effective way of instilling enthusiasm in parents for altered methods, and getting them to apply them in their home, is for them to *see* their child performing newly acquired skills at school. As an extension of review meetings and home visits, some practitioners urge the wider use of direct parent training. Again the parents' flat is useful if a mother is to spend a few days living at the school, first observing her child, perhaps through the one-way mirror of the observation room, performing new desired behaviours, and then learning from the teacher, therapist or psychologist how to elicit these new skills herself. At Ingfield Manor parents of the physically handicapped are required to learn and then to teach basic physical skills this way. Similarly, the parent of the hearing-impaired child who is suspicious of Total Communication could see its value by observing her child using it with her teacher and fellow pupils, to persuade her to learn signing herself. The overprotective mother of the visually handicapped child could observe her child cooking or walking unaided around the grounds and around the local environment, showing an independence the parent had not thought possible, thereby encouraging the mother to take more risks when her child next comes home.

Where the families are in agreement, parent training at school would be followed up by extended visits by staff to the home while the child was living there. Sometimes the staff member would stay overnight with the family, occasionally for longer, helping the parent transfer newly learnt child-management skills to the home situation. Further regular 'check-up' visits might be made at regular intervals to boost morale when progress seems limited or to suggest modifications to schemes in the light of experience. Carefully planned practical guidance of this nature is likely to be more effective than the traditional counselling which tends to be the major ingredient of much home visiting.

PREPARATION FOR INTEGRATION OR LEAVING

Increased joint working between parents and school staff is likely to be required if the child's progress is such, or home circumstances have improved sufficiently, that the child can be integrated into his local day school. In the months leading up to the child's transfer it might be advisable for the child to spend more weekends at home. The parents might also need help and encouragement to arrange a visit to the new school. Perhaps the child's classteacher or the school social worker could accompany the family.

Parents of children attending schools whose numbers may be falling should be on their guard to check that previously honest and helpful staff are not deceiving themselves when they give their reasons why the child who has made good educational and social progress should not return to his local day school. Concern for a school's continued existence can cloud objectivity. However, the psychologist or social worker who is likely to be involved in the review procedure will usually advise the parent when doubtful practice of this nature might be occurring. Conversely, the parents should check that their advisers are not saying that their child is ready to return to a day school, against his teachers' advice, merely to save the LEA money. It will sometimes be wise to try the child back in the mainstream for a short period while reserving a place for him at his old residential school, in case the school's fears were correct.

If the child is to stay at the boarding school until he reaches school-leaving age, then joint planning for his career should take place ahead of his last year at school. Staff should meet parents to ensure that they know what the possibilities are. Have they made contact with the Careers Office? Have they established what suitable courses exist at their local technical college, or perhaps at special residential colleges elsewhere in the country? Do they know where and how school-leavers claim benefits? Some schools despatch the child's teacher or school social worker or senior RSW to visit the home and perhaps to take parents to meet the Careers Officer or other adults who will be of assistance to the youth.

AFTER CARE

Given the wide geographical distribution of their former pupils and the usual financial constraints which hamper the work of residential establishments, the amount of direct help a school can give to its leavers and their families is likely to be limited. In years to come, perhaps schools will rearrange priorities to ensure that at least one experienced member of their staff can devote a significant part of his work to them for the couple of years after leaving school which many youths and their families find difficult.

Where possible, this task is better taken on by professionals living in the child's home town who are able to call round to advise and arrange practical help on a regular basis. However, families do have a right to call on the staff of the child's old school for limited help and the child's former teachers and RSWs should feel an obligation to do what they can to assist. Without a degree of follow-up much of their hard labour with the child over a period of years might be undone and a youth's former unsatisfactory behaviour might re-emerge. The leaver and his family should feel that they are still able to rely on the school for some support.

DOES DISTANCE FROM HOME MATTER?

Closeness of a boarding school to the family home will usually be desirable and should facilitate home–school liaison. However, a family living near a motorway and with access to a car, or even if relying on transport provided by local authority staff, can find it almost as quick to drive to a school sixty miles away as across a tangled network of busy city streets to the authority's own 'community-based' school. Criticisms that rural schools are isolated and inaccessible to families becomes less convincing when a school provides transport to and from home for its pupils in the school minibuses and can despatch an RSW or teacher in the school car to fetch parents for visits. However, the country school must be prepared to spend heavily on motoring expenses to provide this necessary service.

IN THE FOCUS OF HIS FAMILY

Given the wide range of special needs for which residential schools cater, the type of service needed for families is going to differ considerably. Life-skills, behaviour modification or physiotherapy programmes put into operation by parents in their own homes, aided by school staff, might be applicable to children with learning difficulties or physical handicap, but not for most older disturbed children of average or above average ability. For these, regular contact between staff and parents for the two-way exchange of information and to plan the child's future together is likely to be all that can be realistically achieved.

Whatever the family and the child's needs, a competent field social worker on the staff will be an asset in achieving this close home–school liaison. Attention has already been drawn to the excessive demands made of social services department workers. Most recently the Fish Report noted some parents' perception of the inadequacy of the social work support they had received.[8] The Warnock Report of 1978[9] and the Schools Council Report of 1980 on the education of disturbed pupils,[10] made similar points. In contrast, the Fish Committee stressed the usefulness and popularity of the service provided by *school-based* social workers.[11]

There seems to be general agreement that both parents and school staff come to value the flow of information which results if there is a member of staff who can make regular home visits, representing the parents' point of view to doubting staff and justifying the school's programmes for the child to a perhaps suspicious family. It is a potent means of breaking down distrust, dispelling mutual ignorance and winning the support of adults who might have been very critical and distrustful of all the education or social services workers they had encountered before the child's entry into boarding school. Parents have a right to know what their child is doing, what problems he is encountering and how he is progressing. Sparse and bland school reports or snatched telephone chats are no substitute for a well-planned home visit by a capable and respected social worker. One north-eastern residential school managed to finance the employment of two part-time social workers as well as an experienced senior full-time worker, such was the value the managers attached to their work. It was felt that, given the teaching and to some extent the care commitment of education staff, it was not possible for them to concentrate adequately on field social work. Moreover, teachers are not trained for this role.

However, the teachers were encouraged to visit the family homes of the children in their classes, and to act where possible in the teacher-counsellor role advocated by both the Warnock and Fish Committees. Many other schools also involve both social worker and teachers in work with the family home. This two-pronged strategy does help to avoid any potentially dangerous departmentalism, and makes communication more direct. But it can be ineffective and lead to misunderstanding if the social worker, untrained and inexperienced in classroom techniques, is expected to instruct parents on how to put into operation educational and behavioural programmes designed by teachers.

In conclusion, school social workers and teacher-counsellors should aim to make a school welcoming and encouraging to parents; to keep the child in the focus of his family, and encourage parents to show a continuing interest in the pupil's education; to work to help the child fit more comfortably into life in his own home and neighbourhood; and to prepare for and oversee his smooth transition back into his family and perhaps to his new college or place of work.

NOTES

1. M. Ross, 'Mainstreaming: Some Social Considerations', *Volta Review*, January 1978, p. 27.
2. S. Gregory, *The Deaf Child and His Family*, George Allen & Unwin, London, 1976, p. 140.
3. The Education (School Information) Regulations, SI 630 (1981).
4. Gregory, *The Deaf Child and His Family*, p. 141.
5. S. Apter, *Troubled Children, Troubled Systems*, Pergamon, New York, 1982, p. 183.
6. P. Young and C. Tyre, *Dyslexia or Illiteracy?*, Open University Press, Milton Keynes, 1983, p. 156.
7. M. Jones, *Behaviour Problems in Handicapped Children*, Souvenir Press, London, 1983, p. 29.
8. Committee Reviewing Provision to Meet Special Educational Needs, *Educational Opportunities for All* (Fish Report), ILEA, London, 1985, para. 2.14.54, p. 164.
9. Committee of Enquiry into the Education of Handicapped Children and Young People, *Special Education Needs* (Warnock Report), Cmnd. 7212, HMSO, London, 1978, para. 14.23, p. 271.
10. M. Wilson and M. Evans, *Education of Disturbed Children*, Methuen, London, 1980, p. 197.
11. Fish Report, para. 2.14.55, p. 164.

9

The Case for the Special Boarding School

What, then, does the future hold for residential special education? In Chapter 1 DES statistics were quoted showing the decreasing use of boarding schools except for children with emotional and behavioural difficulties and one or two extremely rare conditions. Five factors point to the continuation of this trend:

- It seems certain that, as the school population continues its spectacular decline, some schools will become redundant.
- Given the financial difficulties under which local authorities work and the expense of boarding provision, officers are likely to discourage the transfer of children with less severe difficulties who in the past would have boarded.
- Arguments in favour of extending comprehensive education to all children with special educational needs, harnessed to belief in the disadvantages of segregation of children in boarding schools, will lead to more children remaining in or returning to ordinary day schools. This seems particularly likely for children with physical or sensory disabilities and no pronounced learning or behavioural difficulties.
- If more secondary schools adapt their curriculum and organisation in order better to meet the needs of disturbed children, and if these changes are accompanied by improvements in the effectiveness of non-residential social services intervention (see Chapter 2), less children will need to board.
- Finally, given advances in medical research, the number of children with physical and perhaps learning and behavioural difficulties may

decrease. For example, it has been suggested that 'if available knowledge and best practice were fully applied', 40 per cent of the cases of cerebral palsy, the most common form of physical handicap, could be prevented.[1]

Some day all this might come about and residential special schools will become the dying breed suggested near the end of Chapter 1. However, given present economic, medical, educational and social factors, many of which have been outlined in the early sections of this book, this remains a distant prospect. At least in the interim, many residential special schools will continue to have a role to play.

This was clearly recognised by the 1985 Fish Report which urged carefully planned, *gradual* progress towards full integration.[2] The Committee warned against hasty, under-resourced, piecemeal schemes. While there should be a time-scale for change, the central sections of their report hinted at caution and slowness. Most LEAs seem likely to follow this approach.

The Report acknowledged that there was still the need for widespread curriculum and organisational change in many mainstream schools before they could cater adequately for many children at present in segregated provision. Perhaps reflecting these shortcomings, a greater percentage of schoolchildren attended ILEA special schools in 1984 than in 1976.[3]

Further, they noted that a primary school made great efforts to adapt itself to the needs of the handicapped, only to find parents of the five-year-olds without disabilities opting for other schools.[4] Although an unconfirmed report, this hints that wider mixed ability teaching and alterations to traditional forms of organisation might not be popular with the majority of parents whose children do not have special educational needs.

In similar pessimistic vein, the Committee seems to doubt the capacity of social services departments to provide satisfactory non-residential alternatives to boarding.[5] In confirmation of the acute and increasing crisis in British family life, they record that a quarter of ILEA pupils live in single-parent families.[6] If this statistic is considered alongside the increasing divorce and illegitimacy rates, it seems probable that the overworked and underfinanced social services departments will have to spread their thin support to even more households under intense stress. In view of these social patterns, probably reflected in most centres of population, the number of children with emotional and behavioural difficulties does not seem likely to fall.

Given the financial pressures under which the health service and medical research centres operate, it seems realistic to take a pessimistic view of the advance of medical knowledge or primary health care. It is therefore likely to be many years before the number of handicapped children at present in boarding schools can be reduced substantially by these means.

Thus, all the major reasons suggested in Chapters 1 and 2 for placing children in boarding schools will continue to obtain for the forseeable future.

In addition, the continued existence of many residential schools will be aided by the natural inertia of people employed in the present system. The majority of these will not share the moral fervour of keen integrationists. The latter may have won over much of the media but have yet to convince many experienced practitioners or parents that, in practice, children with special educational needs at present in boarding schools would be better served by 'mainstreaming'. Some professionals will be aware of the difficulties experienced in various countries in integrating children with emotional and behavioural difficulties or profound hearing impairment. They might argue that whatever the *moral* and *egalitarian* arguments, it is unwise to disrupt an established special school network, whatever its faults, for an alternative whose superiority is not established on a firm empirical base. Supporting this position are various figures given in the Fish Report indicating that the majority of parents are satisfied with their children's placement in special schools. For example, 80 per cent of a sample of parents considered the special school successful or very successful in developing their children's strengths and were pleased or very pleased with their progress.[7] Some parents actively pressed for their children to attend special schools,[8] believing them superior to ordinary school alternatives.

Maintaining a choice of integrated and segregated provision is therefore important. For the vast majority of children with special needs, day provision, possibly as part of their local comprehensive system is likely to be preferable, but families should not be denied the option of a segregated alternative, sometimes residential, which might, in their particular circumstances, better meet their family needs. When examining this possibility, parents and the professionals involved should consider the following criticisms, already mentioned in the text above, which are sometimes made of boarding schools and which might be applicable to their particular situation. However, they should also think of the responses which can be made.

Boarding separates the child from his family and interferes with the natural pattern of a child's growing up with his parents, brothers and sisters.

For the child from a loving, stable family, not undergoing stresses outlined in Chapter 2, perhaps this is so, although the many thousands of families whose children attend residential public schools do not seem to think this a drawback of overriding importance. Boarding schools can ensure that, through frequent weekends at home, holidays and communication by phone and letter, parent and child stay 'in tune' with each other and a child does not feel rejected. If the family is under severe pressure, and parent and child perhaps have an uneasy relationship which is full of conflict and problems, then termtimes apart can help to create a happier, healthier relationship and rekindle dormant affection.[9] If family difficulties are not resolved, at least periods apart relieve pressure and give the child the chance to grow up and develop his own personality and interests in an environment which will be free from the trauma he might associate with home, and which perhaps better meets his emotional and social needs. This will be achieved without stigmatising the child or his parents as much as taking him into care of the local authority.[10]

Boarding isolates a child from his local community.

In most cases, yes. But are some children with physical disability ever truly integrated into their local community, given the location of their houses and the extent of their handicap? The Warnock Committee recognised that some severely handicapped children might have to board in order to receive a reasonable range of 'recreational and leisure opportunities.'[11] The maladjusted child from a tangled family background who has been negatively labelled and rejected by other children and families in his neighbourhood might also be isolated.[12] Such children can find companionship in boarding school and make lasting friendships. Even if these can only be enjoyed during term-time, might these not better meet their needs than a lonely life at home?

Boarding denies a pupil a normal childhood, mixing and growing up with local children in ordinary day school.

This statement suggests that the child would be happy in an ordinary day school and benefit from the experience. In fact the majority of boarders with special needs have spent many years in integrated educational settings, have not enjoyed the experience, have been isolated, or have been labelled 'failures' by staff and peers, have fallen behind in lessons and sometimes shown disruptive behaviour or played truant. In contrast, many prosper in the small, segregated environment of the residential special school and have little wish to be reintegrated. If such children had remained in a day setting their continuing isolation and rejection could have been very damaging to their development. It has yet to be proved that mixing children without handicap with pupils with special needs increases the sympathy and understanding of the former for the latter and some evidence suggests the contrary.[13]

Small boarding schools cannot provide the width and variety of the ordinary secondary school curriculum, and therefore limit the educational opportunities and achievement of their pupils.

For some children, as for Angie (see p. 1), this is true; but generously staffed and larger residential grammar schools exist for bright children with physical and sensory disabilities to counteract this criticism. Some schools for the maladjusted arrange for pupils to attend local day schools for subjects not adequately covered by the school's own staff.

Further, is this criticism relevant for the majority of special boarders who have learning difficulties? Would they actually receive a wider education if they attended their particular local day school where they might be placed in an on-site special unit, special class, or withdrawn from other lessons for remedial work in basic subjects? Importantly, would their motivation for learning be as good if they attended their local comprehensive whose size and ethos might do little to encourage the less able child? Pupil self-esteem and resulting motivation for learning are much influenced by how a child's *immediate* classroom surroundings shape his perception of his teachers and peers attitudes towards him. Might not the pupil with learning difficulties in a mixed ability group be attributed low status by his peers and respond with lack of effort, disruptive behaviour or truancy? While there is conflicting evidence one should not overlook those studies pointing to the low self-concept of less able children in non-streamed schools and the high self-concept of those in segregated provision, where teachers and peers are probably more sympathetic.[14]

In some instances, the well-run residential school's concentrated special facilities, homogeneous teaching groups and additional staffing enables curriculum to be more effectively tailored to individual learning and self-esteem needs, enhancing a pupil's opportunities and achievement.

Residential schools can be uncaring, institutionalised places, where children's emotional and social needs are neglected. Even in a flawed home environment, these needs would be better met.

Sometimes, yes. The quality of child care can vary considerably. However, schools with committed, experienced staff paying attention to the many concerns of this book will not be guilty of this.

The special boarding school can cocoon a child in an overprotected community, divorced from the harsh reality of the outside world.

Sometimes, yes. Boarding schools must attack this tendency by adopting those curricula and methods of organisation, suggested in earlier chapters of this book, which keep a pupil in touch with the wider world and prepare him for leaving residential school.

Placing a child in a community where all his peers have similar and perhaps worse difficulties surrounds him with unsatisfactory role models, and possibly leads to the exacerbation of his problems.

Perhaps, for example, hearing-impaired boarders do reinforce each others' immature behaviour.[15] Staff should be aware of this danger and counteract this criticism by means of an education and care curriculum which encourages the development of age-appropriate behaviour. Similarly, the worst schools for the disturbed may be 'universities of crime', but they do not have to be. Millham *et al.*[16] found that, for the young offender at least, this depends upon how successful the staff are in penetrating the 'child-world' and inculcating pupils with their own values. Style of organisation, staffing levels and degree of adult commitment are important factors. In busy, happy, well-organised schools, the role models presented by peers may be more desirable than those of the 'significant others' in a child's life in his neighbourhood and at his old day school. In his former situation, he might have been part of a deviant sub-culture where the environmental pressure to exhibit disturbed and possibly delinquent behaviour was much greater.

Attending a special boarding school might lessen a young person's employment prospects.

Empirical evidence on this topic, as on many others, is lacking, but it can be argued that the stigma attached by local employers (and also by parents) to a child's attending a special class, on-site special unit or the local 'daft' (ESN) school can be much greater than his attending a school at some distance from home, which is not well known in a child's neighbourhood and does not have the perhaps unflattering local reputation of the day alternatives. Before mass youth unemployment, attendance at Approved Schools did not seem to harm a young person's job prospects.[17]

The expense of placing a child in a special boarding school is not justifiable.

Boarding schools are expensive to maintain but LEA and most independent schools are much cheaper to run than CHEs run by social services departments. As argued in Chapter 2, options which link day-school attendance to community-care strategies, properly organised, staffed and of sufficient intensity and duration, are not always significantly cheaper, if the costs to health, education *and* social services departments are considered.[18] Further, it should be asked whether such alternatives meet the needs of a particular child as well as a carefully selected special boarding school?

Also to be put in the balance when considering whether special boarding might be the best approach for a particular child are the positive accounts of the residential approach. Many of these are small-scale studies, the *opinion* of groups or individuals, or the case histories of pupils which of course cannot be accorded the weight of a much needed national survey. Nevertheless, they should not be overlooked, and they do hint that, were large-scale research projects into the work of the best boarding schools to be instigated, a favourable, if qualified, picture of the residential approach would emerge.

Cohen recorded the impressive reading and maths gains which can be made by boarders.[19] Coker's small-scale study comparing the educational progress of the visually handicapped in segregated boarding and mainstream settings suggests the greater success of the former.[20] The improvements brought about in the cerebral palsied boarding in Hungary by following the strict behaviourist programmes devised by Peto and his followers cannot be ignored.[21] Neither can the praise for the successful work of some boarding schools for disturbed children noted by the Schools Council Survey.[22] Cohen and Fillipczak record impressive educational gains made by teenage offenders following a behaviourist programme in whose early stages money was paid for academic progress.[23] Weinstein recorded the social and educational improvements in pupils who attended residential 'Project Re-Ed' programmes.[24]

British Deaf News, the organ of the British Deaf Association, fights strongly for the continuance of boarding schools for the hearing impaired[25] and some parents in the United States have battled to send their children to residential schools for the deaf against the wishes of the local school boards.[26]

Malcolm Jones tells of the impressive improvements in Emma and Trevor, two children with severe learning and behavioural problems.[27] Jo Campling, while recounting the restrictive, under-challenging boarding experiences of Angie (see p. 1), also records the stories of Sarah, a physically handicapped child who had an unhappy experience in a comprehensive school but found greater contentment and companionship in boarding school, and of Micheline, who likewise had unhappy day-school experiences, jumped at the chance of residential placement, where she said for three years she underwent a 'slow healing process'. Similarly, Lisa, another physically handicapped teenager, talked of the lively, varied social life and challenging physical education programme she pursued while she studied for her A levels at Lord Mayor Treloar School.[28]

Mary Wilson and Mary Evans described the opinions of children in three boarding schools for disturbed children. In each they found children who thought their school a friendly place. They were not ashamed to tell their friends at home that they went there, and they worried if their school got a bad name.[29]

A modest study I carried out into the attitudes of eight pupils attending a junior school for maladjusted boys and girls showed these young people's positive view of their boarding school.[30] On a self-image test, the highly disturbed Janet (see p. 2) after eight months in her residential school, saw herself as less quarrelsome, more reliable, polite and popular. Her classteacher believed she was happier, kinder and more honest. Janet appreciated the relationship she had developed with her teachers and with her RSWs. She was proud of the progress she had made in swimming, and of learning to play table tennis, but more importantly, after her very unhappy day-school experience, valued making more friends in boarding school.

Of the other people mentioned at the start of Chapter 1, Darren enjoyed his boarding-school career, making steady if unspectacular education progress, and was able to leave council care. Paul likewise flourished, gaining in confidence, and educational and social skills. His parents fought against the local authority's desire for him to return to day school. Alex, despite one serious relapse, when in the holidays he shot and wounded a neighbour with an air rifle, worked hard for a grade 1 in CSE woodwork, and was accepted into the army soon after leaving. In his last year at school he had changed from a sullen, resentful and defiant youth into a responsible and helpful young man. Tommy and Jason, described in Chapter 2, also found security and some success in residential school.

Similarly, some highly respected authors, after weighing up the pros and cons, recognise the continuing usefulness of residential schools for some children in certain circumstances. To Gulliford, they were 'a great asset permitting the rehabilitation of many children who would otherwise founder'.[31] The National Children's Bureau saw them as a 'legitimate' approach which did not sever the links between child and family and carried less stigma than taking a child into the care of a local authority.[32] Stott noted the shortcomings of fostering and preferred residential schools as a means of helping some maladjusted children. He noted that children could be very happy in them, and were provided with opportunities for friendships with peers and experience of 'caring and devoted adults'.[33] Wilson and Evans clearly approved of some boarding schools for the disturbed. The final chapter of Robert Laslett's useful book, published in 1977, provides encouraging reading for supporters of the therapeutic approach.[34] He reports a few studies which show sound educational progress and reduced maladjustment in boarders. Michael Reed recognised that, for some deaf children, boarding schools 'could be their salvation'.[35]

A carefully balanced view is given by Quigley and Kretschmer on boarding schools for the deaf in the United States. They criticise the assumption that institutional life necessarily produces emotional deprivation in a child. They quoted one, admittedly unusual, piece of research which showed that children living in an institution where excellent child care took place developed *more satisfactorily* than children living at home with their families. They conclude that if good child-rearing practices are followed, and a stimulating, relevant curriculum provided in a warm, affectionate atmosphere, development 'is in no way retarded by educating children in residential schools'.[36]

They also point out the advantages of the centralised and necessarily residential establishment for children with rare impairments. These include the large number of pupils on roll. This reduces the need for mixed age teaching and allows the employment of a large number of teachers who are able to provide a wide curriculum. It is also easier to provide efficient specialised services such as audiology, psychology and social work. The provision of a wide-ranging social and physical education programme is also facilitated.[37]

The above paragraphs do not hide the fact that there is a shortage of empirical evidence proving the worth of boarding. There is also very little showing its failings. The Warnock Committee was aware of this, and recommended that research projects be instituted to clarify its role.[38] Three major areas merit examination. First, what criteria should be used in deciding which children should enter residential schools? It seems likely that the criteria suggested in the Warnock and Fish Reports and echoed and developed in this book will be confirmed, but it would helpful to check this. Second, what learning experiences and educational and social work methods benefit which children? Research which clarified some of the issues discussed in previous chapters would be of great use to practitioners and could make for a more effective service. Finally, what criteria should be used to distinguish the poor from the good residential school and to measure that ill-defined but necessary concept 'success'? In this last respect, criteria commonly applied in the past are inappropriate. Recidivism in leavers from Approved Schools was one such method. This was never satisfactory in that it labelled the leaver who shoplifted a bar of chocolate and was caught by the police as a failure, while the leaver who committed murder but escaped detection was a success. Gaining employment was, until quite recently, another criterion used. When in 1984, according to the Fish Committee, only 11 per cent of children with learning difficulties and 15.9 per cent of children with emotional and behavioural problems obtain full-time work[39] largely because of mass unemployment, this can no longer be valid. Reintegration into mainstream education has been made a top priority by others.[40] But if some parents *wish* their children to stay in segregated provision, and if mainstream schools are imperfect places, perhaps not meeting children's needs as well as the good residential school, is this logical?

If a major research project were instigated, it would do better to evolve or refine instruments which measured children's cognitive, social and emotional advances made *at school*. The detailed assessment schemes already existing in some behaviourist schools might be useful in this respect. Progress made by children while boarding could be compared to control groups in day settings. Research, from a phenomenological perspective, which sought out the opinions and perceptions of boarders and their families would also be useful.

An attempt should also be made to establish how well gains made at school are transferred to the home situation. The emphasis should be more on weekends and holidays spent at home, than after leaving school. A parent of a ten-year-old child in boarding school is more likely to perceive a school's success in terms of how it is helping his son's development and the family situation at the present time, rather than looking ahead to how he fares at home when he is seventeen or eighteen years old. It sometimes happens that a boarding school's contribution to solving *present* problems, and providing a disturbed individual with at least a happy and fulfilling childhood, is ignored and the school condemned because the youth poses problems to society sometime after he leaves school. Gauging a school's success by the fate of its leavers is often unfair. It might have no control over the chance encounters or mishaps which might befall the former pupil. When a younger child knows that he is returning to school after a short holiday is over, he remains susceptible to staff influence, and it is therefore permissible to judge a school by how well his family functions during his vacation. However, allowance must still be made for adventitious happenings and family factors.

The previous paragraph points to the difficulty of identifying reliable and fair variables to use in measuring the effectiveness of the residential approach. However, such problems should not deter schools from keeping honest, detailed records of children's performance in educational, social and emotional areas at school, and at home during holidays and after leaving. Such data might not satisfy the careful scientist, but is better than no facts and figures on a school's performance. It might be worthwhile for such information from a wide range of boarding schools to be collated and made public. Information of this nature, while not carrying the weight of a major national research project, could be useful in identifying more clearly which approaches work for which children, and also highlighting areas in need of remedy.

That there is room for improvement in many boarding schools is not in doubt. This book has indicated important areas where weaknesses continue to lie. These include poor physical provision, underresourcing, friction between care and education workers, unsuitable curriculum, 'warehousing' child care, overstrained and undertrained workers and inadequate co-ordination between staff and underinvolved parents.

Many schools, however, exhibit few if any of these shortcomings.

Such weaknesses are not inherent in the residential approach and should not be used as reasons to deny this service to the parents and children who would, on balance, benefit from it. Educating a child with special needs in a boarding school is seldom the ideal solution and residential special education will not achieve the status or attractiveness which public schools can have for the well-to-do. However, as many parents and pupils acknowledge, boarding placement can be a pragmatic 'second best' which eases many problems while helping a child's education, social, physical and emotional development more effectively than the day school and other local-based alternatives open to him. Even in the long term when as many as possible of children with special needs are being educated with their peers in ordinary primary and secondary schools, a variety of special boarding schools is still likely to be needed as part of the range of special educational provision. For many of the children described in this book, boarding school will remain the 'least restrictive environment' in which they can live and learn.

NOTES

1. J. Loring and M. Holland, *The Prevention of Cerebral Palsy*, Spastics Society, London, 1978, p. 17.
2. Committee Reviewing Provision to Meet Special Educational Needs, *Educational Opportunities for All* (Fish Report), ILEA, London, 1985, para. 3.18.17, p. 192.
3. Ibid., para. 1.4.21, p. 25.
4. Ibid., para. 2.6.39, p. 51.
5. Ibid., para. 2.14.53, p. 164.
6. Ibid., para. 1.2.5, p. 9.
7. Ibid., para. 2.13.33, p. 144.
8. Ibid., para. 1.5.9, p. 34, paras 2.13.29–30, pp. 143–4.
9. A similar idea is expressed in D. Stott, *Helping the Maladjusted Child*, Open University Press, Milton Keynes, 1982, p. 65.
10. R.A. Parker (ed.), *Caring for Separated Children*, Routledge and Kegan Paul, London, 1980, p. 54.
11. Committee of Enquiry into the Education of Handicapped Children and Young People, *Special Educational Needs* (Warnock Report), Cmnd. 7212, HMSO, London, 1978, para. 11.40, p. 216.
12. Stott, *Helping the Maladjusted Child*, p. 112.
13. See studies quoted by K.P. Meadow, *Deafness and Child Development*, Arnold, London, 1980, p. 168; for an outline of other writings on this issue, see O. Eggleston, 'Comparison of the Academic Progress and the Socio-Emotional Characteristics of Segregated and Non-Segregated Slow Learning Pupils', unpublished dissertation, University of Bristol.
14. J.B. Thomas, *The Self in Education*, NFER, Slough, 1980, Chapter 6.
15. S.P. Quigley and R.E. Kretschmer, *The Education of Deaf Children*, Arnold, London, 1982, p. 93; Meadow, *Deafness and Child Development*, p. 96.
16. S. Millham, R. Bullock and P. Cherrett, *After Grace, Teeth*, Chaucer, London, 1975.

17. Ibid.
18. R.G. Walton and D. Elliott (eds), *Residential Care*, Pergamon, Oxford, 1980, p. 3.
19. H. Cohen, 'The Academic Activity Program at Hawthorn', *Exceptional Children*, vol. 30, 1963, pp. 74–9.
20. G. Coker, 'A Comparison of Self-Concepts and Academic Achievements of Visually Handicapped Children Enrolled in Regular School and in a Residential School', *Education of the Visually Handicapped*, vol. 11, no. 3 (Fall 1979).
21. H. Sharron, 'Walking Abroad', *Times Educational Supplement*, 12 July 1985, p. 16.
22. M. Wilson and M. Evans, *Education of Disturbed Pupils*, Methuen, London, 1980, Chapter 6.
23. H.L. Cohen and J. Fillipczak, *A New Learning Environment*, Jossey-Bass, New York, 1971.
24. L. Weinstein, 'Project Re-Ed Schools for Emotionally Disturbed Children: Effectiveness as Viewed by Referring Agencies, Parents and Teachers', *Exceptional Children*, vol. 35, no. 9, 1969, pp. 703–11.
25. *British Deaf News*, May 1983 and July 1984.
26. G. Holman, 'Due Process — A Status Report on Schools for Deaf Children', *American Annals of the Deaf*, vol. 2, 1980, p. 92.
27. M. Jones, *Behaviour Problems in Handicapped Children*, Souvenir Press, London, 1983, Chapters 4 and 9.
28. J. Campling, *Images of Ourselves*, Routledge and Kegan Paul, London, 1981, pp. 1–8, 23–7.
29. Wilson and Evans, *Education of Disturbed Pupils*, Chapter 6.
30. B.E. Cole, 'The Use of Residential Education to Improve Pupils' Self-Image', unpublished dissertation, University of Newcastle upon Tyne.
31. R. Gulliford, *Special Educational Needs*, Routledge and Kegan Paul, London, 1971, p. 9.
32. Parker, *Caring for Separated Children*, p. 54.
33. Stott, *Helping the Maladjusted Child*, p. 38.
34. R. Laslett, *Edducating Maladjusted Children*, Granada, London, 1977.
35. M. Reed, *Educating Hearing Impaired Children*, Open University Press, Milton Keynes, 1984, p. 95.
36. Quigley and Kretschmer, *The Education of Deaf Children*, p. 33.
37. Ibid., p. 42.
38. Warnock Report, para. 18.15(viii), p. 322.
39. Fish Report, para. 2.10.11, p. 105.
40. K. Topping, *Educational Systems for Disruptive Adolescents*, Croom Helm, London, 1983, Chapter 1.

Appendix

Table 1. Number of Maintained and Non-Maintained Special Schools Making Boarding Provision and Number of Boarders, by Handicap, England and Wales, 1983.

	Maintained		Non-Maintained		Total		Percentage of pupils in special education
	No. of schools	No. of boarders	No. of schools	No. of boarders	No. of schools	No. of boarders	
Blind	2	109	12	529	14	638	88
Part sighted	1	235	2	140	3	375	29
Blind/part sighted	0	0	3	220	3	220	68
Deaf	6	176	5	433	11	609	54
Part hearing	2	110	2	251	4	361	74
Deaf/part hearing	7	147	6	676	13	823	42
Deaf/part sighted	1	77	0	0	1	77	71
Physically handicapped	19	491	17	723	36	1,214	18
Delicate	21	1,045	5	250	26	1,295	44
Delicate/physically handicapped	8	189	2	109	10	298	7
Delicate/maladjusted	4	190	1	44	5	234	69
Maladjusted	111	3,555	20	968	131	4,523	47
ESN(M)	95	4,381	9	605	104	4,986	9
ESN(S)	22	443	0	0	22	443	2
ESN(M/S)	7	223	0	0	7	223	4
Epileptic	1	27	4	486	5	513	99
Speech defect	2	44	4	169	6	213	77
Autistic	2	25	0	0	2	25	15
Multi-handicapped	1	23	1	45	2	68	5
Total	312	11,490	93	5,648	405	17,138	

Source: DES, *Statistics of Education*, 1983, Table A19.

Table 2. Number of Boarders, by Handicap, 1973, 1978 and 1983

	1973			1978			1983			Percentage change 1973–83
	Main-tained	Non-Main-tained	Total	Main-tained	Non-Main-tained	Total	Main-tained	Non-Main-tained	Total	
ESN(M)	7,773	1,126	8,899	6,060	752	6,812	4,347	598	4,945	−44
Maladjusted	3,070	1,031	4,101	3,638	1,152	4,790	4,232	1,135	5,367	31
Physically handicapped/delicate	3,407	1,924	5,331	2,211	1,521	3,732	1,639	1,049	2,688	−50
Deaf/part hearing	816	1,765	2,581	773	1,563	2,336	493	1,114	1,607	−38
Blind/part sighted	628	1,261	1,889	544	1,089	1,633	329	890	1,219	−35
Others	167	568	735	839	790	1,629	747	668	1,415	92

Placed by LEAs in independent schools (mainly boarding)

	1973	1983
ESN(M)	1,087	486
Maladjusted	3,515	4,376
Physically handicapped/delicate	874	716
Deaf/part hearing	383	412
ESN(S)	0	703

Sources: DES, Statistics of Education, 1973, Tables 30, 34; 1978, Table 26; 1983, Table A22.

Table 3.   Number of Boarders, by Sector, 1961–84

	Maintained	Non-Maintained	Total	Pupils placed in independents*	DES tables
1961	12,523	7,734	20,257	3,008	(17/20)
1971	15,055	7,657	22,712	4,655	(32)
1975	18,216	7,671	25,887	6,589	(31)
1979	13,495	6,782	20,277	7,477	(28)
1983	11,787	5,454	17,241	7,293	(22)
1983	10,589	4,963	15,552	6,971	(20)

* mainly boarders

Suggested Further Reading

CHILDREN WITH PHYSICAL DISABILITIES

E.M. Anderson, L. Clarke and B. Spain, *Disability in Adolescence*, Methuen, London, 1982.

E. Cotton, *The Basic Motor Pattern*, 2nd edn, Spastics Society, London, 1980.

E. Cotton, *Conductive Education and Cerebral Palsy*, Spastics Society, London, 1975.

HEARING-IMPAIRED CHILDREN

K.P. Meadow, *Deafness and Child Development*, Arnold, London, 1980.

S.P. Quigley and R.E. Kretschmer, *The Education of Deaf Children*, Arnold, London, 1982.

M. Reed, *Educating Hearing Impaired Children*, Open University Press, Milton Keynes, 1984.

VISUALLY-IMPAIRED CHILDREN

E.K. Chapman, *Visually Handicapped Children and Young People*, Routledge and Kegan Paul, London, 1978.

D.J. Harvey (ed.), *Children who are Partially Sighted*, Association for the Education and Welfare of the Visually Handicapped, 1980.

D. Tooze, *Independence Training for Visually Handicapped Children*, Croom Helm, London, 1981.

CHILDREN WITH READING DIFFICULTIES

P. Young and C. Tyre, *Dyslexia or Illiteracy?*, Open University Press, Milton Keynes, 1983.

CHILDREN WITH MODERATE LEARNING DIFFICULTIES

M. Ainscow and D.A. Tweddle, *Preventing Classroom Failure*, Wiley, Chichester, 1979.
W. Brennan, *Curriculum Needs of Slow Learners*, Methuen, London, 1979.
K. Devereux, *Understanding Learning Difficulties*, Open University Press, Milton Keynes, 1982.
A.E. Tansley and R. Gulliford, *The Education of Slow Learning Children*, Routledge and Kegan Paul, London, 1960.

CHILDREN WITH SEVERE LEARNING DIFFICULTIES

M. Jones, *Behaviour Problems in Handicapped Children*, Souvenir Press, London, 1983.

CHILDREN WITH AUTISTIC TENDENCIES

M.P. Everard (ed.), *An Approach to Teaching Autistic Children*, Pergamon, Oxford, 1976.
B. Furneaux and B. Roberts, *Autistic Children*, Routledge and Kegan Paul, London, 1977.

CHILDREN WITH EMOTIONAL AND BEHAVIOURAL DIFFICULTIES

S. Apter, *Troubled Children, Troubled Systems*, Pergamon, New York, 1982.
R. Laslett, *Educating Maladjusted Children*, Granada, London, 1977.
D. Stott, *Helping the Maladjusted Child*, Open University Press, Milton Keynes, 1982.
M. Wilson and M. Evans, *Education of Disturbed Children*, Methuen, London, 1980.

CHILD CARE

Advisory Council on Child Care (DHSS), *Care and Treatment in a Planned Environment*, HMSO, London, 1970.

F. Ainsworth and L.C. Fulcher, *Group Care for Children*, Tavistock, London, 1981.

J. McG. McMaster (ed.), *Skills in Educational and Social Caring*, Gower, Aldershot, 1982.

LESSENING THE NEED FOR BOARDING EDUCATION

Committee Reviewing Provision to Meet Special Educational Needs, *Educational Opportunities for All* (Fish Report), ILEA, London, 1985.

N. Hazel, *A Bridge to Independence*, Blackwell, Oxford, 1981.

B. Holman, *Kids at the Door*, Blackwell, Oxford, 1981.

K. Topping, *Educational Systems for Disruptive Adolescents*, Croom Helm, London, 1983.

K. Widlake, *How to Reach the Hard to Teach*, Open University Press, Milton Keynes, 1983.

Index